# SO YOU WANT TO BE A LESBIAN?

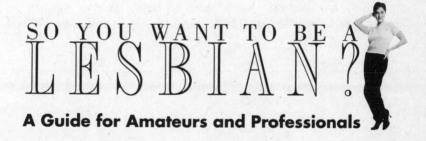

## A Guide for Amateurs and Professionals

**Liz Tracey and Sydney Pokorny**

Original photography by Valerie Shaff

St. Martin's Griffin
New York

DESIGN BY: JAYE ZIMET

Library of Congress Cataloging-in-Publication Data

Tracey, Liz.
    So you want to be a lesbian / Liz Tracey and Sydney Pokorny.
    p.   cm.
    Filmography: p. 143
    Includes bibliographical references (p. 195)
    ISBN 0-312-14423-7
    1. Lesbians—United States.  2. Life skills. I. Pokorny, Sydney.
II. Title.
HQ75.6.U5T73   1996
646.7' 008' 6643—dc20                                96–3340
                                                     CIP

20  19  18  17  16  15  14  13  12  11

# SO YOU WANT TO BE A
# LESBIAN?

# ACKNOWLEDGMENTS

To my parents, for teaching me to stand up for what I believed, even when it flew in the face of everything they thought was right; my brother and sister for putting up with my smart ass; Hunter College High School, for turning out such fabulous lesbians; ACT UP–New York Class of 1989; *Outweek* magazine, especially Michelangelo Signorile, for giving me a place to write and therefore alienate every woman who ever read our fine magazine; the young people at the Hetrick-Martin Institute: I learned more from you than you'll ever know; *Out* magazine, especially Michael Goff, Elyse Harris, and Sarah Pettit; Routledge, especially Jason, Stephanie, Darren, Todd, and Cecelia; my agent Victoria Sanders; Keith Kahla: An editor with a sense of humor is a very good thing; Alison: To my Good-For-Everything Girlfriend. Finally, to Dorothy Allison and Pat Califia: You probably don't remember this, but you held me down and signed my boxer shorts once, and I love you every day for it.

—L.T.

My share of this book is dedicated to the memory of my father, whose death I don't think I will ever fully comprehend, and to my mother, whose love, patience, and strength have been a constant (and I might add, underappreciated) comfort. Thanks and eternal gratitude to Liz and Victoria for coming up with and selling this book. Extra special thanks to everyone at *Artforum* who put up with me for so long (don't know how), especially to David who has always been there to provide much needed support and guidance. To Amy D. who is the strongest, wisest, and wittiest person in the whole fucking universe, thank God I know you and I can never thank you enough for everything that you've given me. Thanks also to Aimée and Oliviu for liking the same bands I do and never missing a show. A huge thanks to everyone in the AOL Hole and Queer Punk folders who provided info on bands and zines that I couldn't have done without. Much gratitude is also owed to Chip

Duckett, Michelangelo, Michael Musto, Michael Wakefield, Violet, Stacey, and the Prom Queen, who have all offered support and inspirations at various times through the years. And to Eliot, Alex, and JM who I love and miss beyond all words.

—S.P.

To our glamorous models, who braved cold weather, Avenue D, and stage fright to pose for the photographs in this book—Laura Stine, Jaye Zimet (also a fabulous designer), Stephanie Schwartz, Mikel Wadewitz, Amy-Lynn Fischer, and Ann Northrop: You rock our world. (One of the authors is in here, too, but it would look really self-serving to thank ourselves for just showing up.)

# CONTENTS

This book came from an idea that came to a friend of mine who is full of good ideas, Cecelia Cancellaro. She envisioned a series of how-to books for various subcultural identities, *How to Be a Lesbian Performance Artist*, or *How to Be an Anarchist*, etc. . . . You get the idea. A few months later, *So You Want to Be a Lesbian?* was born, and you're holding the result in your hot little mitts.

In approaching the subject, the idea was never to write a book for people who aren't lesbians. It was to give those who are some fun reading material, a little practical advice and perhaps some insight along the way. If nonlesbians are reading this, it doesn't mean you should give up. The humor here is, we hope, broad enough that you can enjoy it, too—just remember though, laugh with us, not at us. (We'll know the difference.)

It's amazing how much more there is out there now—films, music, literature, and resources—than even five years ago. There has been a boomlet in dyke culture, and, believe it or not, there wasn't enough room to include everything. Any omissions are ours, and we don't pretend to know everything. The keyword here was "eclectic," not "exhaustive," or "scholarly." And yes, we were hoping for some laughs.

The reactions we got when telling people about it were cautious: A few laughed, some outright condemned it, and most said they would reserve judgment until they actually read it. So, for the Doubting Thomasinas, we're eagerly awaiting your opinions.

We hope you enjoy reading this as much as we did writing it. Saying much more would detract from the book itself. So stop slogging through this and get in there.

Liz Tracey
December 1995
East Village, New York City

# SO YOU WANT TO BE A
# LESBIAN?

# Test Your LQ™
# (or, the Lesbian Aptitude Test [LAT])

Here's one test you shouldn't have to study for. Answer each question as honestly as you can (and don't look at the answers; we'll know if you've cheated). You'll find the scores at the end of the test.

## I. In Utero

**1.** When your mother was pregnant with you, morning sickness was most aggravated by:

A) TV sporting events
B) Food
C) Engelbert Humperdinck
D) Anita Bryant

**2.** During her pregnancy, your mother most craved:

A) Kentucky Fried Chicken
B) Pickles
C) Frozen yogurt
D) Granola and soy milk served in a handmade ceramic bowl from Guatemala, bought to help the United Grapeworkers Union

**3.** Of your birth, you remember:

A) Absolutely nothing
B) Being slapped
C) The light at the end of the tunnel
D) Thinking "Oh my God, I am *never* going to do this when I grow up."

## II. The Childhood Years

**4.** When playing house, you were:

    A) Mommy homemaker
    B) The idiot son, Doug
    C) Betty, the beautiful and popular daughter
    D) Daddy, with the girlfriend on the side at the "house" down the street

**5.** When choosing up sides for sports, you were:

    A) Picked first
    B) Picked last
    C) Team captain
    D) Behind the wall with Betty from "playing house"

**6.** When picking out stories for "current events," you chose:

    A) Stories of great political import
    B) "Lost Puppy found in well" stories
    C) Sports scores
    D) Feminists protesting various misogynistic cultural events

**7.** On graduating, your principal said you had a future filled with:

    A) Great promise
    B) A happy marriage
    C) A great career
    D) Various female "roommates" and a cat named Gertrude

## III. High School/College

**8.** At dances you were:

    A) DJing/playing with your band, Black Reign
    B) Drinking vodka in the schoolyard with the football team
    C) Playing poker in the cafeteria
    D) Sneaking up to the science lab with the new cheerleader

**9.** Which character from *90210* were you most like?

A) Brenda
B) Andrea
C) Donna
D) Kelly
E) Dylan

**10.** In college, you were active in:

A) Stop Rape Now
B) Junior Achievement
C) Divestment from South Africa
D) Queer Nation (but only as a "civil rights" issue)

**11.** Your best friends were:

A) Your roommates
B) Phi Gamma guys
C) Your sorority sisters
D) The girls from the field-hockey team

**12.** Two-part question:

Did you ever attend a sorority party?

A) Yes
B) No

If so, which of the following statements best sums up your experience?

A) "God, it's amazing how there's a direct correlation be-tween blond hair and IQ."
B) "I don't know about your pledging; we tend to have very high standards here at Tri Delta."
C) "I cannot believe one small girl could drink that much."
D) "Oh, God, I never knew it could be like this with a woman!"

**13.** You majored in:

A) Women's Studies
B) Animal Husbandry
C) Art History
D) Bisexuality

## IV. Adulthood

**14.** Your first job was working as a:

A) Temp
B) Go-go dancer
C) Commodities trader
D) Clerk at the local health food co-op

**15.** Your favorite night spot is:

A) Mingles
B) Bennigan's
C) I don't go out—I'm spiritual.
D) Clit Club

**16.** When you rent movies with a new friend, the first thing you watch together is:

A) *Beyond the Valley of the Dolls*
B) *Walk on the Wild Side*
C) *Entre Nous*
D) *The Hunger*

**17.** Which character are you most like on *Melrose Place*?

A) Jo
B) Alison
C) Amanda
D) Sydney
E) The blond one who's so boring, no one can remember her name anyway
F) Billy

**18.** You were rooting for:

    A) Tonya
    B) Nancy
    C) Oksana
    D) Anyone in the short track speed-skating competition

**19.** Your favorite sport is:

    A) Tennis
    B) Football
    C) Synchronized swimming-team event
    D) Watching Gabrielle Reese in those Nike ads

**20.** Complete this sentence: "My ideal relationship is best embodied by":

    A) Jean-Paul Sartre and Simone de Beauvoir
    B) Gertrude and Alice
    C) Beavis and Butthead
    D) k.d. and Martina

# SCORING KEY:

1. a=0; b=1; c=2; d=3
2. a=0; b=1; c=2; d=3
3. a=0; b=1; c=2; d=3
4. a=0; b=2; c=1; d=3
5. a=1; b=0; c=2; d=3
6. a=2; b=0; c=1; d=3
7. a=1; b=0; c=2; d=3
8. a=2; b=0; c=1; d=3
9. a=0; b=2; c=1; d=0; e=4
10. a=1; b=0; c=2; d=3
11. a=1; b=2; c=0; d=3
12. Part 1: a=0; b=1
    Part 2: a=3; b=2; c=1; d=4
13. a=3; b=1; c=1; d=2
14. a=1; b=3; c=0; d=2
15. a=1; b=0; c=2; d=3
16. a=2; b=2; c=1; d=3
17. a=4; b=1; c=2; d=3; e=1; f=-4
18. a=2; b=0; c=1; d=3
19. a=1; b=2; c=0; d=3
20. a=0; b=3; c=1; d=2

If you scored:

**0 to 22:** Sorry to break this to you, but we're surprised you managed to figure out you're a lesbian. But luckily, you're an insightful, sensitive person who has found this book. There is hope yet.

**23 to 43:** You are someone with varied interests and is not afraid of going her own way.

**44 to 65:** You are probably a lesbian overachiever. Perhaps you might want to introduce some elements of other subcultures into your life in a quest to broaden your horizons.

## 1. There are homosexual recruiting offices located in New York, San Francisco, and other secret locations throughout the United States.

Actually, Lesbian-Americans are born, not made.

You can't just show up and declare your intention to defect. It's not like we're a refuge for the heterosexually disaffected. There are rigorous tests, which must be passed. Along with an aptitude test (see: "Test Your LQ™," p. 1) you must take three of the following Lesbian Board Tests:

▼ Women's Studies
▼ Riot Grrrl-ology
▼ Queer Theory
▼ Vegetarianism
▼ Cinema Studies
▼ S/M/B/D(I/O/U)
▼ Interpretive Women's Music Dancing
▼ Feline Veterinary Medicine
▼ Body Modification
▼ Mechanics (Motorcycle or otherwise)
▼ Arts and Crafts
▼ Fashion (high or thrift store)

The applicant may choose those tests which best suit her abilities and areas of life concentration. After passing, there is a secret initiation ritual, not unlike a Bat Mitzvah combined with a baptism, except instead of becoming a woman, you are now a woman-identified woman. Then you go to Provincetown to celebrate.

## 2. All lesbians want to be men.

Hmmm, let's see. . . . Men get paid a whole dollar for a woman's sixty to sixty-nine cents. They get more bathroom accommodations, better service on airplanes, paid attention to in electronics stores, don't get sexually harassed on the street, aren't laughed at when playing sports seriously, and have no equivalent terms like "bitch" and "ho"—gee, let's revise the above statement in light of these facts:

All *women* want to be men. At least for a day.

### 3. There's always a man and a woman in a lesbian (or gay) couple.

Again, another simplification used to oppress us and to make it easy on straight people who can't deal with complexity. This awful stereotype has kept queer people down for centuries.

The truth is: In every lesbian or gay couple, there is one who is Mary Tyler Moore, and the other may be one of four characters:

▼ **Rhoda:** The hip, happening partner with an artistic side who helps Mary get through the rough spots, and is there to share the joy when she's happy. Doesn't necessarily need to be from New York City, but it helps.

▼ **Lou Grant:** Gruff but lovable, a subtle, yet real source of support for Mary. While this combination is often rocky romantically (see the episode where Mary and Lou go on a date), if it works, both Lou and Mary find real love and succor in one another.

▼ **Murray:** The solid breadwinner, the worrier, the *mensch*. Loves Mary dearly and puts her on a pedestal. Unless his gambling problem gets out of hand, this can be a wonderful coupling.

▼ **Sue Ann Nivens:** A match made in hell. Sue Ann will always need to compete with Mary, put her down to boost her own ego because of her intense insecurity, then cook chocolate mousse to make herself feel better. This combination is almost always doomed to failure, because Mary just won't take it for very long.

*Important note:* The phrase "Get over it, Mary" stems from the Mary identification of same-sex couples. When you hear this being used, it is an almost certain indication of which one is "the Mary."

### 4. Lesbians all have bad haircuts.

See The Great Lesbian Haircut Conspiracy, p. 102.

---

## 5. All lesbians have cats.

This is a blatant lie, an untruth, a falsehood. Not all lesbians have cats, because many lesbians have allergies. A lot of allergies, to a lot of allergens. While no conclusive study has been done, one may infer a higher incidence of sensitivity in various lesbian communities from the following facts:

▼ They were the first group of people to use "scent patrols" (or more colloquially "smellers") at events, to sniff out scents that might cause discomfort to attendees.

▼ They pioneered the use of scent-free perfume ("No one knows you're wearing it except you. Live the fantasy. The personal is political . . .").

▼ They chose a rocky Greek Island with little flora or fauna to cause sneezing, runny nose, or sinus headache to name themselves after (Lesbos).

▼ Patchouli, a fragrance that could stop a herd of cattle at fifty feet (thereby fighting its way through blocked nasal passages) is the scent of choice when wearing "a public fragrance."

Those gay women who are allergy-free have a variety of animals, not just cats. So there.

## 6. All lesbians are flattered when compared to Gertrude Stein.

Okay, think about this: Gertrude Stein was a great figure, a pioneering writer, a woman who knew her art and her (soon-to-be-famous) writers. But blasphemous as this may be, it begs to be said: Gertrude was no looker. She resembled a statue *before* she died. Her philosophy of clothing was to buy what was "comfortable and durable"; i.e. painter's canvas with sleeves. We honor her as a matron saint of the arts, but the next time you have the urge to say "Oh, you remind me so much of Gertrude Stein!" think very carefully about what you're saying. Would you be flattered hearing that? Decide and speak accordingly.

## 7. All lesbians wear flannel.

Everybody wears flannel now. So what's your point?

## 8. All lesbians are good at sports.

Yes, that's true, but we trade off our ability to dance in order to beat guys in pool. No, no, no. Using standard elementary logic, it is very simple to disprove this. All lesbians are women.

Not all women are good at sports.

*Quod erat demonstrandum*, not all lesbians are good at sports.

## 9. All lesbians need is one good man, and they'll change their ways real fast.

Please. This is so tired, my grandmother fell off her dinosaur the last time she heard it. Also, have you seen the guys who think they're "the right one"? Ugh. Even Phyllis Schlafly would think twice if she was responsible for repopulating the earth after a nuclear holocaust with one of these slugs.

## 10. Lesbians secretly run the world.

(Damn!)

Well, hmmm . . . I . . . yeah, I guess they do.

So what are you gonna do about it?

# TERMINOLOGY

A GLOSSARY OF TERMS FOR
THOSE IN THE KNOW

**Assimilation:** As advanced by Bruce Bawer in his book *A Place at the Table*, the proposition that either a) we're just like everybody else, so we should be given our rights, or b) we *should* be more like everyone else, so if the drag queens and leather dykes would just get the hell back in the closet, we "normal homosexuals" could get our rights. (Yeah right. Go tell that to Jesse Helms and see how long it takes for you to want to strangle him.)

**Babydyke:** Usually understood to be a young lesbian in her teens or early twenties who may still be learning the ropes. Can be extremely frustrating to the young woman in question, who may feel like punching out the next lesbian she comes onto who says "Oh, you're so cute! You're such a babydyke. . . ."

**Bar Trash:** A lesbian who spends too much time in a bar or club for some judgmental person's liking; could mean they're just jealous of the bar trash's success with the other patrons.

**Bisexual:** A woman whose sexual and romantic orientation is directed toward members of both sexes.

**Boys:** Term of affection used by lesbians to denote their gay male friends.

**Breeder:** Term for heterosexuals. While some straights find this term "homosexist," many queers take delight in doing exactly to them what has been done to us for years.

**Bulldagger:** A term for a butch lesbian, originating among African-Americans. While once an insult, some butch lesbians have claimed it as their own.

**Butch:** A lesbian whose self-identity takes on aspects of the traditionally "masculine."

**Celebudyke:** A lesbian who is famous or near-famous for doing almost nothing. Ingrid Casares, who is known primarily because she has dated her way through the **lesbian elite,** is a prime example. On a local level can refer to a dyke on the scene, whether activist or club hopper, whom everyone knows.

**Cyberdyke:** This can either denote a lesbian who works in the computer or electronic information industry, or someone who spends a great deal of time "online."

**Dinah Shore Golf Classic:** Somehow, this golf tournament in Palm Springs became a yearly girls' equivalent of Sydney's Gay Mardi Gras. Twenty thousand women are estimated to cavort and attend wild parties. A must-attend, at least once, just to figure out what the allure is (see Sports, p. 112).

**Drag King:** The female equivalent of drag queen.

**Drama Queen:** One who can't get through the day with out some trauma, mostly of her own creation, taking over her life, and by extension, those around her.

**Dyke:** Thought of by some as a pejorative term, it has been reclaimed by both radical lesbians of the seventies and the younger activist women of the nineties. This may unfortunately be the only thing they have agreed on recently.

**Dyke Punk:** A lesbian who lives in the punk lifestyle. Come in a variety of girls: **riot grrrl**, **vegan**, crusty (one who wears leather), emo (a sensitive brooding type), and kinky (S/M punk).

**Dyke Tyke:** Men, sometimes gay, sometimes straight, who perpetually hang out with lesbian friends, and aspire to lesbianism as a higher consciousness. The male equivalent of **fag hag**.

**Fag Hag:** Traditionally a straight woman who hangs out with gay men, sometimes in the false belief that eventually she may evince change in them, other times just because they get along very well. More recently, with the boundaries between gay men and lesbians

breaking down, there are more and more queer should⌐
shared.

**Femme:** A lesbian whose self-identity is that of a "feminine'⌐
This is an erotic identity, and not indicative of someone who⌐
comfortable with her lesbianism. Both **butches** and femmes had very
difficult times with straight society, as they were the most "visible" lesbians, thus incurring a majority of discrimination and violence. They
were also dismissed as "mimicking the patriarchy" by their more "androgynous" sisters, who missed the message of subversion in the coupling.

**Galimony:** Descriptive term for what is owed to the "divorced" partner of a rich/famous lesbian, generally in the act of suing for same.
Coined when Billie Jean King and her former lover became the test
case.

**Gay Male Wannabee:** A lesbian who identifies with gay male culture.

**Gay Woman:** Used by: women who think "lesbian" sounds like a
bad disease (see **internalized homophobia**); yuppie women who
feel they have more in common with closeted gay men who make
$100,000 a year than their less privileged sisters; women in the Mid-
west who are just generally happy.

**Girl:** A term used among lesbians (younger) to denote themselves.
Should not be used unwisely by men, unless among friends.

**Girljock:** Named after a magazine of the same name, but means a
dyke who participates in the subculture of lesbian sports.

**Girlsloth:** A lesbian slacker. (There is no magazine, as none of them
could get up enough energy to finish the first issue.)

***Hothead Paisan:*** The ongoing serial comic by Diane DiMassa,
published by Stacy Sheehan, that tells the story of Hothead, a homicidal lesbian terrorist, and her cat, Chicken. Must have. The best answer for assimilationists.

**Internalized Homophobia:** The inherent discomfort with one's
sexual orientation that is formed by society at large. Can be manifested
in many ways, primarily in **assimilation**.

**Leather Dyke:** A lesbian who either participates in the leather/S/M community, or just dresses like she does.

**Lesbian:** Named for the Isle of Lesbos, where Sappho, the mother of us all, wrote poetry for cute young Greek **girljocks** and vied for their affections. Denotes a woman whose sexual and romantic orientation is directed toward women. Some women prefer lesbian to **gay** because the latter has become so synonymous with men.

**Lesbian Chic:** This may have been brought about by the rise of the **lipstick lesbian**. Depending on who one speaks to, it was either a) a great leap forward for lesbians everywhere, with big magazine spreads and buzz galore, or b) a heinous co-optation of our culture by the usual suspects in an effort to defuse any advances made, and an opportunity to gawk at us as usual. (In all honesty, the whole thing probably lasted about three weeks.)

**Lesbian Elite:** An everchanging list of dykes in the public eye who have come out. There are certainly national members, as well as East Coast and West Coast affiliates (think of it as a major television network and you have the general idea). National: k.d., Martina, Melissa, Ingrid, Jenny Shimizu (model), Madonna (on reserves list). East Coast/West Coast: Dorothy Allison, Susie Bright, Pat Califia, Diane Di-Massa (*Hothead Paisan*) Jenny Livingston, Sarah Schulman, Rose Troche, Guinevere Turner. (This list has monthly updates, check your local press for current standings.)

**Lipstick Lesbian:** A lesbian, generally **femme** but not always, who wears lipstick and/or other makeup and has a certain flair for designer clothes and champagne. This may also involve ritual worship of Coco Chanel and Sandra Bernhard.

**Nancy Girl:** A seemingly asexual woman who hangs out with lesbians, but has never been seen or known to have carnal knowledge of anyone. Could be coming to terms with her sexuality, or a **wannabee** in hiding, or simply someone with no luck getting dates.

**Queer:** Another term which started out as "pejorative," now reclaimed by both younger and/or radical gay men and lesbians of the late eighties and early nineties. Those who favor it do so because they find it more inclusive, covering **lesbians,** gay men, **bisexuals, transgendered** people, S/M people, etc. Those who abhor it either find it still too negative, or otherwise don't want to be subsumed into such a long list of identities.

**Riot Grrrl:** A young feminist activist; may or may not be lesbian.

**Running-shoe Lesbian:** Lesbians, usually over thirty-five, who wear jogging shoes with everything (also called a yuppie dyke).

**Straight Queer:** From the seminal article by Ann Powers in the *Village Voice* (1993). Stands for those who are heterosexually inclined, but who live primarily in the queer sphere. Those who are confused by this, join the club.

**Transgendered:** A person who may or may not have had gender-reassignment surgery, but is living as a member of the opposite sex. They may or may not believe in the bipolar gender system, and as such "transgendered" connotes a living across the divide, as it were.

**Vegan:** One who not only practices vegetarianism, but who eschews any products made with animal furnishings.

**Wannabee:** When used by a lesbian, a pejorative term for women who may or may not identify as lesbian, but who don't sleep with other women, but expend all of their cultural energy in lesbian venues. When used by a wannabee, this is a term of homage "Oh, I wish I was a lesbian, but I guess I'm just a wannabee."

# CLOTHES MAKE THE WOMAN, OR, SOME DEFINITIONS BASED ON DRESS

**Armani Dyke:** Just what it sounds like, except it doesn't have to be Armani. A woman, probably of means (or whose partner has means) who dresses in extremely fashionable suits, with tasteful accessories, and a haircut which requires some form of upkeep. Often reminiscent of the Paris lesbians of the 1920s, except they're not in Paris and no one speaks French. (Note: This type can be either butch or femme, depending on accessories and presentation.)

**Gap Dyke:** Buys her clothes primarily at the single most heinous clothing chain in the universe, or one of its sister stores (Old Navy or Banana Republic). Specializes in commonsense clothing whose effect is that of looking like a mid-range creative type at an advertising agency (like Andrew Shue on "Melrose Place," except without the square shoulders). Primarily butch, because femmes care way too much about clothes to wear Gap women's clothing.

**Boiler Suit Dyke:** This may be more popular in England, as it's almost unheard of in the US. Immortalized by Edina (Jennifer Saunders) in *Absolutely Fabulous*, when pleading with her daughter to be a lesbian so she would be more interesting. Her parting line, "Why don't you wear a boiler suit and get a haircut. . . ."

**Laura Ashley Dyke:** A *rara avis*, but these are the same lesbians who worship Martha Stewart and bake their own nontraditional Winter Celebration ornaments. Often femme to the point of almost being undercover lesbians, Laura Ashley types need a great deal of cash flow for upkeep and equipment. The positive side will be the envy of your friends at the marvelous entertaining you do.

# Coming Out

How often we of the same-sex affectional persuasion hear the words: "You know, people would be much more tolerant of gays and lesbians if they wouldn't talk about it so much." (You can also substitute things like "flaunt it," "throw it in our faces," and other choice phrases which actually all mean "if you would get back in your closets, we'd all breathe easier.")

But what fun is it to be this special and not share it with anyone? Some people describe the self-awareness of knowing and accepting your sexuality as the sort of thing you want to shout from rooftops. (Don't do this right off the bat—see below.) You want to tell people your happiness. Walking around all the time in a state of heightened excitation can become apoplectic for you and extremely annoying to others: "*What?* What is it already? Just tell me, Jeez. . . ." The other concern, touted by both political action groups and individuals alike, is that coming out can change your life and the views of those around you.

There is no ideal time to come out. Some women are "born out" (and believe this: They won't let you forget it—"Yeah, I was dating my first woman in junior high school. . . ."), but some women don't come

## FIVE THINGS YOU SHOULD DO BEFORE COMING OUT:

1. Actually sleep with another woman.
2. Check with your local Lesbian Draft Board to make sure they're not over quota for the month.
3. Make sure you can drink herbal tea without gagging.
4. Buy some politically conscious T-shirts and wear them *all* the time.
5. Pick an interesting method of transportation (motorcycle, four-wheel drive vehicle, bicycle, Birkenstocks) and stick with it.

out until their fifties or sixties. You'll know when you're ready to tell other people about it—and there are as many coming-out stories as there are out lesbians.

Each situation (or each person) requires a personal approach that you will know best. There are very good resources for people who are thinking about coming out to parents, families, and friends (see Resource Guide, p. 203), and using these along with your common sense will make the experience a little less stressful (more like having your arm hair ripped off with packing tape, as opposed to having all your body hair pulled out with tweezers).

However, not everyone feels like she needs to be out. That's a choice—no one should pressure you to do it. If someone is trying to tell you to do it, tell them to take a hike, and you'll do it when you're good and ready. There have been a few instances of "accidental" coming out—"Whoops. I just came out to Aunt Martha and she passed out in the strudel." If this happens, do not panic. Assess the situation, and act accordingly (first thing for Aunt Martha is picking her out of the pastry). But trust your instincts.

## "No, Mom, I didn't say 'Lebanese'"

Parents are usually the last to know, although anecdotal evidence supports that they are the first to suspect. After you've told all your friends and roommates, maybe stray ex-boyfriends, you feel ready to move on to the Big One. Some things to think about when approaching the subject:

▼ What sort of reaction am I expecting?

▼ What if that isn't the one I get?

▼ Is there any reason that I should be worried about doing this?

You should *seriously* consider:

▼ Do I have somewhere to go if this doesn't go well?

▼ Will I have to find other means of financial support?

▼ Are there people in my family I care about (siblings, nieces/nephews) I may lose contact with if this goes badly? Will other family members feel the same way they do?

You may weigh these issues and come to the conclusion that it's better to wait. If you do come out to them, be aware of a number of reactions that aren't necessarily common, but do occur:

▼ **Selective Hearing Loss:** "What was that, dear? I'm sorry, I didn't hear you." "Mom, I'm gay." "Yes, it is, isn't it, dear?" "What?" "A nice day. It's a lovely day." "Mom, no, no, no, I'm gay. I'm a lesbian." "No, we're not. You're Welsh, just like the rest of us. Your mother looks Italian, but I just think maybe there's a little Irish in her." "(strangling noises) No, Dad, not Lebanese. . . ."

This could go on forever. And in some cases it might: the nice parental equivalent of "I'm not having it!" Sometimes they'll break and let you know they've known all along, and this is just how they have chosen to deal with it. Or, it could be just a phase they're going through.

▼ **"We're So Happy for You!"** While this isn't always the first reaction, many parents (especially those who fancy themselves liberals) will move into a seemingly harmless joy that their daughter has taken up such a revolutionary life-style—and there's the problem. Sure, it's great to have your parents try to set you up on dates (how accepting they are, and thoughtful too), but no one straight, gay, or otherwise wants to go out with someone their parents pick out. Eventually it may come out (so to speak) that your parents are patronizing you, and really in the back of their minds are thinking that you'll grow out of it. Just give them speech No. 3: "No it's not a phase. Really. I mean it. . . ." (no foot stomping; it kills the appearance of maturity) and make them deal. You'll soon know if they are.

▼ **Concerned and Informed:** This is similar to "We're So Happy," but with less of a condescending tone, and more of an uncertain acceptance. These parents are identified by their reading of books on queer history and culture that even you haven't read, keeping up with the various anti-gay bills coming up in state referendums, and their never-ending letter writing to your hometown paper complaining about their coverage of lesbian and gay issues. If you are sure that your parents are motivated by what they feel is doing the right thing, then you have a wonderful, natural-born ally, as well as a great conversation topic: "Well, my dad doesn't think the Idaho bill's going to pass. He thinks if anything, Ohio's the next one to go." "Your *dad* said that?" "Yeah, he's the head of Stop Hate Montana." "Wow!"

▼ **Trying to Save You from Yourself:** These parents could totally drive you out of the house and up the wall. After you've come out to them, they will stop at nothing to try and fix you up with a man. Repairmen will suddenly be ambushed by your mother, carrying a loaded

Bundt cake, asking him if he's seeing anyone special. Your phone number will suddenly in appear in phone booths near sports bars. Never once will they ever come out and say "We can't stand that you're a lesbian." This one isn't so funny after the fifth time a guy with bad hair and a box of chocolates shows up at your door, saying "Your mom said. . . ." You need to end this FAST.

▼ **Grandchildren: By Any Means Necessary:** These are parents who have only one thing on their minds: baby booties. Grandkids. They want little tykes (or dykes, even) to read stories to, and coddle and spoil and complain about baby-sitting for. When you came out to them, it barely phased them. "Right, you're a lesbian. But you still want kids, right?" "Yes, I do." "Great, okay, when?" "When what?" "When kids?" "Heck, Dad I'm nineteen!" "I know, Kitten, I just want to make sure I'm still here when little Sappho or whatever you're going to name her gets here." You're afraid to have a girlfriend over to their house, because they start sizing her up. "Hmm. She's tall. Excuse me, Greta? Do you have a brother? Good. Has he ever thought of becoming a sperm donor?" "*Mom!*" You can either continually bash your head against the wall of their single-minded determination for you to give birth in the next possible moment, or perhaps humor them, even get back at them. Go over during a holiday and bring a bunch of home-pregnancy tests. Make sure you go to the bathroom often. Feign nausea. This might even stop them.

# DOS AND DON'TS
# OF COMING OUT:

▼  DO check for emergency exits.

▼  DON'T wear your Aileen Wuornos T-shirt while coming out to your parents.

▼  DO smile. A smile is a good way to disarm people (so is karate).

▼  DON'T pat them down before talking to them. This may set a needlessly antagonistic tone.

▼  DO make sure that they're perfectly clear about what you're telling them. This prevents abrupt and sometimes painful future conversations about what it is exactly that "sapphic" means. ("No, it's not like hyperactive. . . .")

▼  DON'T describe your first night of passion with a woman in detail with those who don't ask first. Too much information can make the coming out process much more painful and overstimulating than it has to be.

It's entirely possible that all of your friends already know that you're playing on Sappho's team. They've just been tapping their feet, waiting around for you to get a clue and come out. These are probably the best friends to have since your big declaration will make them feel not only closer to you, but superior since they now think they knew before you did. They may even have potential dates lined up for you. This is known as the *best-case scenario.*

More likely, if you're coming out to straight friends, they may not know how to react. If they've been told over and over again that "queers are evil" and "wrong" it's going to be difficult for them to assimilate you, who they obviously like and care about, with what they know about "them," who is now "my friend Sarah."

You can usually, but now always, get an idea of people's potential reaction by listening to what they say. Chances are if every epithet you hear from them is "faggot" this and "dyke" that, they're probably not going to take it well. Someone who's supportive of lesbian and gay civil rights may become a great ally.

But, and this is a *big* but, your enlightened, liberal friend's protestations of support may turn out to be a lot of lip service when confronted with a real live person who makes her/him paranoid. Conversely, your best friends from elementary school may need to see a real live lesbian to break through their ignorance, and your telling them can change their minds.

The key points to remember:

▼ Assume nothing.

▼ Be prepared for a lot of questions.

▼ Be prepared to lose friends whom you thought would be there through anything.

A lot of times, people who have the hardest time with your coming out are people who have their own sexual identity issues to deal with. It's best not to say "I bet you're really upset because you're like me. . . ." This could serve to disrupt completely whatever process of coming to grips they have started. It's possible that down the road, you'll find each other again, and be great friends.

▼ Remember, there are plenty of people who are supportive and can help you with this (see Resource Guide: Coming Out, p. 203, 221.)

▼ It's not the end of the world.

▼ If they're really your friends, they'll come to understand.

▼ If you're really lucky, your friend will come out to you, too. And then you can get married, thereby bypassing the need for dating, breakups and painful involvement with the lesbian demimonde. (Fat chance. Keep reading.)

## FIVE QUESTIONS MEN WILL ASK YOU FOREVER, ONCE YOU'RE OUT:

1. Which one of you is the guy?

2. How can I get lesbians to sleep with me?

3. All of my ex-girlfriends are gay now. . . . Do you think it's me?

4. So what's the deal with Cindy Crawford anyway?

5. My girlfriend's really curious. . . . What are you doing later?

You come out to strangers anytime you are open about yourself in public. If you are out, in essence, you're coming out to new people every day. Most lesbians don't walk up to strangers and say "Hi, I'm Mindy. I'm a dyke. Seeya." (Besides, there are surprisingly few lesbians named Mindy.)

The most likely places you're going to deal with coming out to the public are:

Work
Restaurants
Public transportation
Hotels
Laundromats
School
Restrooms
Clubs
Gas stations
etc.

Actually, pretty much everywhere you go, your sexuality becomes a potential issue, and not because you bring it up (and straight people think *we're* obsessed with sex). All people have the right to disclose as much or as little about themselves as they want. It doesn't make you more queer to kiss your girlfriend at Arby's, but if it is something you want to do, you should have the right to (however, Roy Rogers has better roast beef).

## Postmodern Lesbian:

This type tends avidly to pursue all manner of academic endeavors. The accessories tend toward "chunky": big shoes, big glasses, and often, real big books. Everything else is modeled on an economy of fashion, a sort of neo-Barthian, Lyotard-influenced, pomo/post-fem look, with . . . oh, hell, you know what we mean.

## A GUIDE TO POTENTIALLY
## NERVE-WRACKING EXPERIENCES

There seem to be four methodologies used when confronting either blatant ignorance or willful stupidity on the part of the Straight Nation. These are:

**The Ostrich:** "I am going to pretend this isn't happening and go on with my life."

**The Mary Poppins:** "I am going to make the best of this situation!"

**The Nell Carter** in *Ain't Misbehavin':* "Ain't nobody's business if I do . . ."

(and of course)

**The Lea DeLaria:** "That's right, I'm a BIIIIIIIIIIIIIIG DYYYYYYYYYYYYYYYYYYKE!"

See if you can match the responses to their proper philosophical school.

**Krissy and Tina** are traveling together. They stop for the night at a motel. The clerk gives them a room with two twin beds, and no way to push them together. Should they:

**a)** just be happy that the clerk didn't look like Norman Bates, and try to get some sleep?

**b)** huddle together in one of the twin beds, trying to recapture the furtive allure of teenage sex?

**c)** go down to the desk and request a room with a king-size bed, saying nothing about their status?

**d)** run down to the clerk's desk, and say "Hey buddy, what's the big idea? How am I supposed to sleep with my girlfriend in these kiddie beds?"

In the dead of winter **Mary Sue and Ellen** are walking along the street. Bundled up in their coats, a belligerent flower seller takes them for a straight couple, and harangues Ellen: "C'mon, sir. You don't want your lady to think you're a cheapskate. Come on mister, buy her some flowers. . . ." then follows them halfway down the block, continuing his monologue. Should:

**a)** they laugh it off, and think fondly of the day when things like this won't happen anymore?

**b)** they quietly but firmly continue to walk, uncomfortable about the complex issues raised by the situation?

**c)** Ellen buy the flowers, give them to Mary Sue, and then make out happily in front of the flower guy?

**d)** Ellen say "Hey, that's Mister Dyke to you!" and continue on their merry way?

**Whitney and Lisa** are celebrating their one-year anniversary at a very lovely restaurant near their house. Lisa had called ahead and wanted to surprise Whitney with an anniversary cake. When dessert comes, the only straight waiter in all of New York City stumbles right past them with the cake, decorated with a little bride and groom statue. He completely ignores their table, asking various mixed couples if they are Lisa and Whitney. Should Lisa:

**a)** kiss the cake good-bye, and take Whitney out for dessert elsewhere?

**b)** quietly inform the manager that the cake is theirs, after the waiter has returned it to the kitchen, thereby avoiding a scene in the middle of the restaurant?

**c)** grab the waiter, and remark loudly, "Hey Whitney, it's a good thing you're in drag tonight, otherwise this would be totally humiliating."

**d)** beckon to the waiter for the cake, and kiss Whitney across the table as it's being served?

There are virtues and drawbacks to each approach. You obviously need to decide which is appropriate depending on the situation, how courageous you're feeling, and how many handguns you think are present. As for Mary Sue and Ellen's laughing it off and thinking of a rainbow future, our advice is: Don't hold your breath.

Why should debutantes be the only people entitled to a presentation to society? Sisters should be able to enjoy the same rights and privileges as every other woman, regardless of their financial or societal standing. One suggestion for visibility (and the added pleasure of making conservatives enraged) is throwing coming-out parties. Here's a checklist of how to do "a do" to make your presence in the world known.

### What kind of party?

Are you traditional? Formal? Casual? Will this be a group party or a solo "outing"? Would you prefer a house party, or do you feel like the VFW Hall is a great place to kick loose?

### Who to invite?

Probably a good mix of those who know, and those who you would like to know, but just haven't been able to say those four little words to ("I am a lesbian.") This way, if all the people who are finding out run away, you won't be left alone with the appetizing platters, crying into your bouquet.

### What kind of music?

A key ingredient to any party. Some suggested items are:

"I'm Coming Out"—Diana Ross
"I Am What I Am"—From the original cast album of *La Cage Aux Folles,* or the disco remake
anything by k. d., Melissa, Danielle Brisbois, Chastity Bono, The Communards, Bronski Beat, 7 Year Bitch, Tribe 8, or Whitney Houston
"Glad to be Gay"—Tom Robinson Band
*Lavender Jane Loves Women*—Alix Dobkin (Note: Be very careful playing this or any other "wimmin's" music. What may appear to be rampant homophobia among your guests as they flee may simply be a bad Cris Williamson reaction.)

**Escorts:**

If you have a girlfriend, you're all set. Otherwise, invite five really hunky women as your escorts, and make them get you drinks and dance with you. Remember, it's your night to shine.

You might even want to place an announcement in the hometown paper. Make sure you get a good head shot for the photo. You might want to put your escorts in the photo as well, so you're not mistakenly hounded by the Daughters of the American Revolution looking for new recruits.

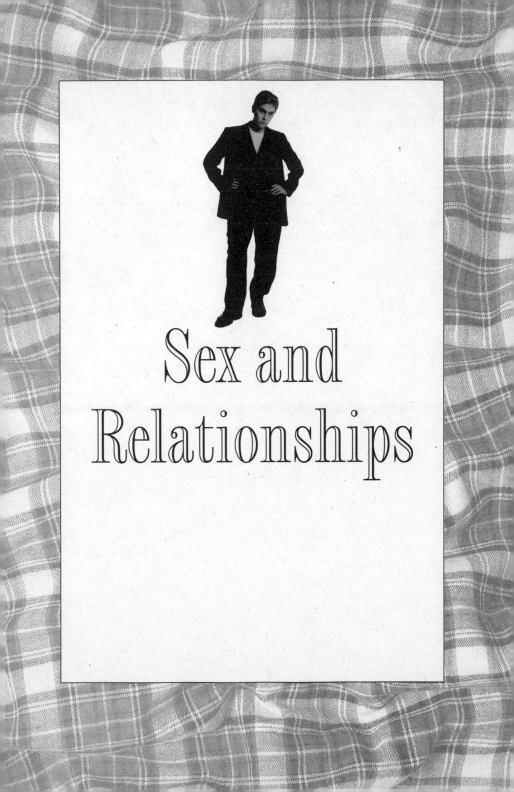

# Sex and Relationships

## First Things First

**Q:** Where would I find women who share my interests?
**A:** Well, dear, if you've come this far, one might assume you've encountered at least one other like-minded woman. However, if you're a novice (or "virgin," in equivalent terms) here are a few places to start, with the pros and cons of each.

### 1. The Local Lesbian/Gay/Women's Community Center or Activist Groups

*Pros:* You'll be in a low-pressure atmosphere. It's not as if anyone is expecting you to put on the first night. You'll expand your horizons by participating in various political and cultural activities. You'll be contributing to your communities. You don't have to wear heels (unless you want to). Nothing's an aphrodisiac like a good protest (ask any ex-hippie: They'll agree).

*Cons:* If other people feel you're there to "scope chicks," they may resent you for cheapening their space. Once you find someone you're interested in, it will take forever to get her alone (hence the term "community"). You may channel so much energy into your horizon-broadening that you'll just be too tired to do it. You'll get into some ugly political situation and be purged. If you meet someone, every single person will follow your relationship like the *Enquirer* on Charles and Di.

### 2. Professional Organizations (e.g. Lavender Accountants)

*Pros:* You'll find people with a common interest *and* occupation. You'll advance your career. You'll find out who else is "on the team," thus giving you gossip for weeks. Professional organizations hold many social events with other professional organizations, expanding your pool of potential suitors exponentially.

*Cons:* You may not want to talk about your job all the time. You may begin to compete with your future girlfriend for jobs. You may begin to hate your profession and be forced to leave and take a job at the Waffle House, finding personal fulfillment but taking a big pay cut.

## 3. Bars

*Pros:* You know why you're there. *They* know why you're there. If you become very nervous, stiff drinks are available. Everybody looks good in disco lighting. There are usually a lot of mirrors, so you can discreetly observe the other patrons. You can pretend not to hear potential unwanted paramours ("What? I can't hear, the music's too loud").

*Cons:* You may find your future girlfriend more attractive having *not* seen her dancing on a tabletop to Pat Benatar. The music can be awful. You may drink too much, leading you to go home with a woman named Hilda, who's just getting over a bad relationship, and is heavily on the rebound. You may waste a great deal of time figuring out if you'll bust a move, just to find her walking out (with Hilda) as you're buying her a drink (see Flirting, p. 41).

## 4. Bookstores

*Pros:* Bookstore pickups have become very popular as of late (cf. *The New York Times* Styles Section). It makes you look smart. Odds are, she can read. You can bump into each other in the "Gay/Lesbian Interest" section, thereby confirming your suspicions. Many bookstores have cafés nearby (or even inside), so you can continue your conversation *à deux.* You can fondly remember "the first time you met" without thinking of beer, smoke, and some guy with a tambourine doing the Hustle with himself to "Enough Is Enough."

*Cons:* If this is *not* a gay bookstore, you may find yourself barking up the wrong tree. If it *is*, you'll probably be holding a video like *Frat Girls Get Spanked* when the love of your life first sees you (however, this could work in your favor). She may be the girlfriend of someone who works there, and you'll never be able to go back until the girlfriend quits. She could be a famous lesbian author, and two years later, you'll find yourself an object of ridicule in her next novel ("Gee, Kate, that sounds like you, except for that part where you sexually assaulted the narrator").

# For Advanced Students Only:
## (Go at Your Own Risk)

### 5. Public Transportation

*Pros:* A fairly low pressure place, once you get past the potential for fatal mistakes. There's a whole world of conversation fodder (the book they're reading, the delays, the gentleman exposing himself on the platform). You can always place an ad in the local "alternative" paper if you lose each other. If it's a complete disaster, you can always get off at the next stop. If you travel to work the same way all the time, you'll get to see each other frequently.

*Cons:* Except for obvious clues (reading Rita Mae Brown, *Out* magazine, or wearing a Lesbian Avengers T-shirt), it's a virtual crapshoot vis-à-vis sexual orientation, and the interested party next to her may be her very large husband. You could be caught in an embarrassing situation and be too humiliated to continue (the vehicle lurches, you touch her breast, turn red, and get off fourteen stops before your destination). Your fly could be open the entire time.

### 6. Laundromats

*Pros:* You can check out her laundry beforehand for telltale signs of hetero male clothing (briefs, not boxers; Henry Rollins T-shirts with the sleeves ripped off; lots of white cotton socks). People are usually looking for a way to kill time while their clothes are washing. You can strike up conversations about her March on Washington T-shirt. You can consolidate your position over fluffing and folding. You know she lives nearby (nobody travels far to do the laundry). If things don't work out, it was just a way to pass the time.

*Cons:* Again, the "is she or isn't she" question arises. Laundromat pick ups are *so* sitcom. The March on Washington T-shirt could be her girlfriend's. If you strike out, you live close enough that you'll run into her again ("Oh, look, there's that rude girl who came onto me at the Disco Laundromat"). She may just be looking for an afternoon quickie (then again, so may you).

## 7. EXTRA CREDIT

▼ Concerts
▼ Grocery stores
▼ ATM lines
▼ Airports
▼ Business conferences

# BAD PLACES TO MEET LESBIANS:

▼ Republican conventions (Republican women's clubs may yield a few prospects).

▼ Countries in which lesbianism is punished by actual physical and psychological violence inflicted by the state (not like the U.S., where they punish us by other, more subtle means).

▼ Interstate diners (no one knows why, it just doesn't happen).

▼ Revival meetings.

▼ Sexually transmitted disease clinics (not that they aren't there, but it's just that you might want to wait until they've finished their medication).

▼ Beefsteak Charlie's/Red Lobsters (simply not a lot of carnivores among the tribe).

# FLIRTING

You have managed to get gussied up in an outfit of your choosing, one that you feel sends the appropriate message to potential suitors. You have dragged yourself to somewhere lesbians gather (see previous chapter), and you have planted yourself firmly in a position to meet and greet. What next?

First, you cry.

"What the hell am I doing? I don't know how to meet a woman! What do I say? How do I say it? How do I know if she's right? How do I know if she's secretly remembering everything I say so she can tell her friends over there what a jerk I am? Ohmigod, that cute blond is looking at me . . . shit."

Relax. Breathe into the nearest paper bag and listen up:

▼ *Don't look desperate*—this is bad. Not that you can't *be* desperate: You're horny, you're lonely, you're in need of companionship, you don't want to waste that Sarah McLachlan ticket—these are all common feelings. Just don't wear them like the rank limburger-like odor that they are.

▼ *Do look friendly.* It's like your mother said,[1] "People will talk to you if they think you're a nice girl." Sure, the nineties are "No More Mr. Nice Girl" times, but it won't get you a date.

   *Smile if someone looks your way.* If you like someone, smile at them. Don't stare, though. This could be taken as potential wacko behavior. Fleeting eye contact made meaningfully is much more effective than hard, stare-down tactics.[2]

▼ *Do talk to people if they talk to you.* Silence is not the proper response in situations like these. Just answer as if

---

[1] They have occasional moments of lucidity. There is no scientific reason for it; sometimes they just know what they're talking about.

[2] The best way to describe this is "smiling quietly" as opposed to "grinning loudly."

you were talking to someone you were introduced to at a party.

▼ *Don't wuss out.* If it seems as if things are going well, don't suddenly remember you forgot to feed your pets. Let them eat cake. A sustained, intelligent conversation is the best way to conduct a flirtation. If she has to leave, ask for a number. Offer yours. If things are going very well, maybe you want to go somewhere more intimate.

Presented below as an educational service are some true dialogues which demonstrate both the Dos and Don'ts of flirting.

# 1

**A:** Hi.
**B:** Hi.
**A:** You're really hot.
**B:** So are you.
   (They kiss deeply for minutes in the middle of a dance floor.)
**A:** You want to go to your house?
**B:** Sure . . .
   (They leave together.)

This almost never happens. But if it does, be forewarned that leaving with strangers is never a great idea. If you're going to do it, make sure you introduce them to someone who knows you. (That way you can also assure yourself of being the object of gossip for weeks afterward.)

# 2

**A:** Excuse me, do you have the time?
**B:** Yeah, it's eleven-thirty.
**A:** That figures. I was supposed to meet someone. I guess she couldn't make it.
**B:** I'm sorry.

**A:** Oh, no. She's always blowing me off. I don't know why I bother.

**B:** I knew someone like that. I couldn't deal with her anymore.

**A:** So what did you do?

**B:** Broke up with her . . .

This conversation is truly ambiguous. There could be subtexts abounding, it all depends on the body language, eye contact, and vocal cues given throughout. Remember, flirting is a full-body sport: It's not what you say as much as how you say it.

## 3

**A:** Hi, can I help you?
(If you're in a restaurant, don't immediately assume you're being flirted with. This could be what some people call "waiting tables." Read on.)

**B:** Yeah, can I have an iced cappuccino, please?

**A:** Certainly. Anything else you'd be interested in?

**B:** I don't know really. . . . Can you suggest anything?

**A:** That depends . . . what's your taste like?

**B:** I'm sort of flexible. (Smiles.)

**A:** I think I can work with that. . . . (Smiles back.)

Again, on the surface a perfectly ordinary conversation. But what lurks beneath could keep you warm on a cold night.

## 4

**A:** Um, hi. I was wondering if maybe I could buy you a drink or something? I mean, if you're not too busy or with anyone, or waiting for someone or something? Because if you are, I really don't mean anything by it, I just thought it would be nice to have a drink or something, or talk to you, I mean I don't want to bother you. . . . (etc.)

Good opening, but she spends so much time trying to seem like she's not doing what she's so obviously doing that you just want to slap her when she comes up for air, and say "It's okay, buy me a drink, flirt with me. I'm all for it."[3]

## 5

**A:** Hey.
**B:** Hey.
**A:** Sex?
**B:** Nah.
**A:** Weed?
**B:** Shure.

(Smoke a couple of big Blunts.)

**A:** Sex?
**B:** Shure.

This is an example of the longterm effects of drugs on lesbians. Sure, it will probably get you laid, but neither of you will remember it, and at least one of you will get a raging sinus infection from continuous exposure to smoke. Figure out what you want most (sex or long term memory loss) and act accordingly.

[3] The few people who can carry this off are the kind who use "aw, shucks" and foot-scuffing as an everyday means of communication. Most jaded, world-weary lesbians seem idiotic trying to effect any innocence. So act like you know.

# BAD FLIRTING

## A PRIMER

We may have been socialized to flirt with men—act coy, play hard to get, don't show you want them when you do. Two women flirting with each other is a verbally erotic act when done well, one almost subversive in its complete exclusion of men, a dance of words and sexual tension (see *The Hunger* or *Go Fish* for good flirting scenes).

When done badly, it's like fingernails on the chalkboard of the libido. You don't recover quickly, and it puts you off the whole topic for a while.

Here are some scenarios to avoid. They are presented only as a caution: The authors cannot be responsible if you take these out and use them in public. Any ridicule incurred will be the sole responsibility of the speaker.

## 1

> **A:** Hi. What's a nice girl like you doing in a place like this?
> **B:** I'm a lesbian. And you?
> **A:** Oh, hah. That's funny. I'm one too.
> **A:** Good. So you'll understand that I don't appreciate being called girl, and come onto like a piece of meat. Furthermore, (etc.).

This isn't so much a bad pickup as a bad choice of pickup. This woman would talk you to death before you ever got to first base. Cut your losses and walk away.

## 2

> **A:** Come here often?

You really don't want to know the answer to this, so don't ask. If you're in a bar, and someone says, "Yeah, actually, I've been coming here

---

five nights a week for the past ten years," it's going to make you wonder.

# 3

**A:** I'm sorry to interrupt you, but I just had to say that you're the most beautiful woman in here, and I would love to get to know you better.

**B:** Thanks. (Goes back to her conversation.)

DO NOT interrupt people to pick them up. Aside from showing a distinct lack of couth, it opens you up to getting dissed majorly by someone who may be involved in a serious conversation with the girlfriend who's breaking up with her because she's a tramp and does any woman who happens by.

Just think, if you'd waited ten minutes, you could have had her like *that*.

While flirting is all about sex and romance and eroticism, the whole point is to not know what it's about right at that moment. Call it subtlety, call it a masquerade, call it denial. But best remember—think before you speak.

# ANATOMY OF A PERSONAL AD

With lesbian and gay liberation making its tiny footsteps forward, more and more newspapers and weeklies in cities and towns all over this great land carry personal ads for the same sex. When approaching the acronym-laden columns of eight-point type, looking for love, it helps to have an interpreter. As a public service to you, the reader and potential ad-placing public, an explanation of commonly used terms can be found below.

**G:** Gay

**W/H/B:** White, Hispanic, and black respectively. (Most papers haven't quite made the jump to African America and Latina yet. If you see "AA" used as an abbreviation, it may possibly stand for "Alcoholics Anonymous.")

**J:** Jewish

**D:** Divorced. While rarely used in lesbian personals, it has appeared. It may also mean dominant, so it pays to read the whole ad before picking up the phone.

**F:** Female. While this may seem obvious in a section labeled "Women Seeking Women," you'd be surprised.

**Bi:** This usually means exactly what it says—bisexual. Sometimes, it means "I'm not quite sure of where I fall on the Kinsey continuum yet, but it would sure be fun to find out." Other times it means "I have a boyfriend/husband and he likes to watch." If you're not up to spectator sports, make sure you know what you're getting into.

**Bi-curious:** This can mean the same as "bi," but in a random survey of personal ads, it has been determined that this is often the lesbian equivalent of "straight-acting" in gay men's ads. To put it bluntly, "I'm in the closet, no dykes." (See "No dykes" below.)

**Fem/Femme:** Enjoys presenting herself or is seeking one who is "feminine" in appearance and role in romantic and sexual relations. (see Butch/Femme, p. 180.)

**Butch:** Enjoys presenting herself or is seeking someone who is "masculine" in appearance and role in romantic and sexual relations.

**Soft Butch:** Either what one might call a femme-y butch, or else she's in the closet.

**Androgynous:** Butch, but doesn't identify as such.

**Feminine:** Not the same as "femme." Usually can be read as "straight-acting."

**(Height, weight, and age):** Whether one includes these or not is completely up to the ad placer's discretion. Sometimes, you will also see requests for people of a particular height, weight, and age as well.

**D/D free:** Drug and disease free.

**No butches:** A commonly seen admonition to women who don't fit a traditionally "feminine" appearance not to even bother. Can mean that a) either the person seeking is butch herself and is very clear about what she wants, or more often b) is suffering from some internalized homophobia and needs to work through this.[1]

**No dykes:** While more modern and/or radical women see "dyke" as a fine thing to be, others still think it means "butch." (see above)

---

[1] It's odd how one never sees an ad which includes the phrase "No Femmes." Go figure.

| | |
|---|---|
| **No fats:** | Beginning, sadly, to make an appearance more and more often in women's ads, this has been a staple in gay men's ads for years. |
| **No men:** | You'd think this would be obvious. Appears mostly in bi women's ads, as a public service to stupid straight guys who might be sorely disappointed on the resounding rejection they will encounter. |
| **No couples:** | Can mean one of two things: that the woman is simply not interested in hooking up with someone with baggage (namely, a girlfriend) or that heterosexual couples looking to swing will need to look elsewhere. |
| **Looking for friendship, maybe more:** | Wants to get laid. |
| **Busty:** | C cup or more. |
| **Top:** | Rarely seen in women's ads, this would denote the "active" partner in sexual activity. Could be a real boon to the woman who claims it, as it's been rumored that there is one top to every ten to twenty bottoms in any area. Doesn't necessarily mean butch. |
| **Bottom:** | Denotes the "passive" partner in sexual activity. |
| **No role-playing:** | Means "no butches," or "no dressing up like a nurse and pretending you're a patient with some vague itch that I have to examine you all over to find." |
| **No tude:** | No attitude. Nonspecific term which means "I'm really fussy, so don't be surprised if I reject you for no good reason." |

A good personal ad conveys just enough about you to get someone interested, and enough about who you're looking for to get them to respond. One rule of thumb is to write a few ads and have your friends read them for honesty and silliness. Anything that makes them laugh at you, not with you, should be tossed. Where you are placing the ad will often determine what it contains as well. If you're placing one in *The Town Crier,* it probably won't be nearly as specific as one placed in *On Our Backs,* especially if it's your hometown crier and everyone will be able to figure out who you are and write you obnoxious fake responses just to be funny.

Most ads have phone response lines and these are good. Some have written responses sent to a mailbox, which can be more interesting, as sometimes people will send photos or other material in the hopes of grabbing your attention. Make sure that when you're meeting people for the first time that you go somewhere public and don't bring strangers to your house. You'll know pretty soon if your date is a loon. Don't give out your phone number or address to anyone if you don't feel comfortable with them. If one of your respondents is the ex-girlfriend you just dumped in a fiery, unpleasant breakup, it's probably best just to not respond at all, rather than tell her, "Hey you responded to my personal ad, which just goes to show how stupid you are since the last thing I meant was for some loser like you to think I would be interested." Muster some maturity and then get out there and have fun.

## SAMPLE PERSONAL ADS AND THEIR INTERPRETATIONS:

**GBF ISO GB/HF** for hot times and good clean fun. NS/D, no roles. I'm 32, diminutive but athletic. Want to meet the woman who can show me what I've been missing. Phone/Photo gets yours.

*Meaning:* Gay black female seeks same or Latina for sex (sometimes in the shower). No smoking or drugs and no butch/femme. Probably more like 35, around 5'1", and has a lot of energy. Last girlfriend couldn't find a fire in Hell, let alone get her off. If you send a photo and your phone number, she'll get to see what you look like, and then decide if she'll send hers.

**Preppy-Wasp Woman:**

Wearing khakis, Top-Siders, and her father's Harvard sweater, this type will enchant you with her sparkling wit, outspoken opinions, and secret debutante past. Sometimes, she can leave you wondering how she ever stumbled across the idea of lesbianism, let alone coming out. But remember where she went to school—chances are we're talking about Seven Sisters.

You've flirted, you may have even dated. But right now you're in an apartment or a house or a hotel somewhere and there's a bed nearby. You're both staring at it. You've been in this situation before or maybe not. Everything you thought you knew about sex just flew out the window. You can't think clearly, since most of the blood in your body has flown south for the impending activities. You're horny. You're breathing heavily, and you're in a panic.

In the great tradition of the twelve-step programs seemingly embraced by our sisters, here is our twelve-step program to having great sex the first time.

1. *Relax:* These aren't the Olympics. You both want to be here or else you'd be reading the section on *Seducing Yourself: How to Be Your Own Best One Night Stand.* Don't think you have to be the best lover this woman's ever had, thereby assuring you'll be so concerned with your performance that no one's going to enjoy it. There's time enough for performance anxiety and she's just as nervous as you are.

2. *Talk:* Talk about what you both enjoy. Ask her what she likes. Tell her what you want. As much as people say "Whatever you like," we all have secret things we *really* love, so why not share? Little things like "I'll come if you suck on my earlobes" can make things so much more interesting.

   Don't forget to talk during sex. Tell her you like it. Tell her if you don't—it doesn't have to be like assembling furniture, but there's no point in doing something that's more annoying than exciting. Afterward, tell her how much you liked it, how hot she is—nobody minds hearing things like that.

   (*Note:* It is probable that during your life, you will run into women who don't talk during sex. This is fine. You can ask them about this after the first time. They won't run away if you do—they'll just think you're incredibly kinky.)

3. *Breathe:* This sounds stupid, but many women have gotten lightheaded and dizzy, a few even passed out cold, because they forget to respirate. **The importance of oxygen during sex cannot be overemphasized.**

4. *Don't expect the earth to move:* This is because a lot of women have difficulty having an orgasm with a new partner or in a new situation. If you don't put a lot of pressure on each other to have (multiple) multiple orgasms, it will be that much easier. However:

5. *Be patient:* Just because we're not pressuring anyone into orgasm doesn't mean you should give up after five minutes. If it feels good, that's what's important. Nothing is better than having someone do something that feels incredible and knowing they'll keep doing it for as long as you want them to. Don't cripple yourself, but remember a little "stick-to-itivness" goes a long way.

6. *Keep the lines of communication open.*

7. *Keep breathing.*

8. *Use your body:* Just as verbal cues are important, so is your body language. If you can't wait for her to touch you, get her there yourself. If you want to be on top, get on up there. Sex should be an experience in which you're fully engaged body and soul.

9. *Laugh:* People don't laugh enough during sex. Taking anything too seriously can rob it of its fun—going to bed with someone is no different. Don't be afraid to do it—it's not a library or a church (God forbid).

10. *Don't be selfish:* Odds are, if you've been getting all the attention, there is a very overheated woman next to you in bed. Make sure to follow the Golden Rule: "Do unto others as you would have done unto you" (unless you've discussed otherwise).

11. *Do not under any circumstances roll over and go to sleep.* This is incredibly tacky, and a guarantee that you'll never get a second invitation.

12. *Don't assume what will happen afterward:* You might be disappointed. Or pleasantly surprised.

## How to Know if You're Having Good Sex

▼ You remember her name

▼ You forget yours

▼ You don't think about how much laundry is lying in the corner of your room where everyone, especially she, can see it

▼ You don't feel as if you want to get up in the middle of it to go shoot pool or bowl

▼ Her gasps of passion did not sound like Tasmanian goat thrashing songs (even if that's what they were)

▼ Your pets go neglected[1]

▼ You forget to eat

▼ You can go for hours without a cigarette and you ordinarily smoke like a chimney

▼ You want a cigarette for the first time in your life

▼ No matter how much her house, habits, or beliefs repel you, it doesn't matter as long as she never stops doing exactly what she is doing at that moment

▼ You're shocked to learn that you missed Pride Day

[1] To animal activists: We are not encouraging this sort of behavior. We deplore letting the kittys and doggies or ferrets or what ever exo-specieal companion one chooses to share one's life with go hungry or unwalked or stuck in a corner of the sofa for three hours because being flexible, one can pretty much curl up wherever one wants. However, it must be noted that on occasion even the most conscientious human companion will abandon one's responsibilities in pursuit of more animal . . . oops, um . . . fleshly pleasures.

We would also like you to know that no animals were used in the creation of this book.

# DATING, SEEING, AND GOING OUT

## AN EXPERT SPEAKS

In an effort to get accurate information on the elusive phenomenon of lesbian dating, we contacted Dr. Melanie Hillgate, a self-acknowledged expert on Sapphic dating practices. She kindly granted us an interview in her spacious home in Santa Cruz, California.

**Q.** Is there actually lesbian dating?
**A.** Yes, there is. Contrary to popular belief, two women don't just meet and get married.

**Q.** What does a lesbian date consist of?
**A.** A short list would include eating, sports, culture, and dancing. However, dancing is often saved for later dates, as no one really wants to scare off a potential suitor with awkward physical movement the first time out, or for that matter, find out their date is a geek on the dance floor.

**Q.** What is the goal of a lesbian date?
**A.** Well, that really depends on who you ask.

One response would be: The goal of a lesbian date is to meet another woman, enjoy her company, and during this process, ascertain whether she is someone you would be interested in pursuing something more serious with. This is known as the philosophical approach.

Another response might be: to meet future sexual partners and perhaps someone for a long-term relationship, while learning more about them and yourself in the process. This would be the pragmatic approach.

Finally, the third response would be: The goal of a lesbian date is to get laid. This is known as being honest (laughter).

**Q.** What happens when a lesbian date goes badly?
**A.** Oh, dear. It would be nice to think that if it went badly, that both women would simply chalk it up to experience and go their separate ways. Alas, it's not that simple.

If both women had a bad time, they probably keep quiet about it, repeat little of it to their friends, feel like failures, and politely avoid each other at social events.

If one woman had a good time, and the other ranked it up there with root canal, the woman who enjoyed it will tell all her friends how great it was and call to arrange a second date. Her calls will go unreturned.

The other woman will have told all her friends how awful it was. "She spilled soup on me and didn't apologize; she took me to a straight bar and insisted on kissing me in front of all these homophobic stock brokers; she took me to bad performance art and made me participate in a ritual roast-beef service"; and will screen all her phone calls. Her friends will tell their friends about "the date" until finally someone will tell the woman who had a great time that in fact, it wasn't all that great and that she has now been placed on the local Lesbian Bad Date Index.

**Q.** Wow. What happens when a lesbian date goes well?
**A.** Logically, other dates will follow. Eventually, the physical tension will be broken and some sexual consummation will occur. With this, the terminology takes on a more complex turn.

If one is dating someone exclusively, but not quite sure where it is going, then you are "seeing" them.

If one is dating someone exclusively, and there has been talk of further escalation on both sides, this is referred to as "going out."

If one is dating someone not exclusively, but sleeping with them on a regular basis, then they are "fuckbuddies."

If one is dating someone exclusively, but seeing someone else behind her back, this is called "cheating."[1]

If one is dating someone not exclusively, and not sleeping with them, then you are "stringing them along."

**Q.** Are lesbian dates different from heterosexual dates, and if so, how?
**A.** Aside from the obvious, there are a few notable differences.

---

[1] (See Monogamy, p. 73.)

---

56

All lesbian dates are dutch, unless otherwise specified.

There may be some confusion when it comes to door opening, chair holding, and other traditionally "male" role-associated behavior.

Sometimes, both parties bring flowers.

Both parties can go to the bathroom together.

The likelihood of their having met at a political brunch, a twelve-step meeting, or a dyke-punk concert are high.

The likelihood of their having met at an "all you can drink Jell-O shot party," a Christian stockbrokers convention, or a Kenny G concert are, thankfully, very low.

Finally, at the end of the evening, no one walks anyone home, unless it's on the way.

**Q.** Are lesbian dates any different from gay male dates, and if so, how?

**A.** While there may be more similarities with gay men than with straight couples, there are still very real differences.

On gay male dates, rarely does anyone talk about k.d., Martina, Melissa, Ellen DeGeneres, Sara Gilbert, Gertrude and Alice, H. D., Virginia and/or Vita, Audre Lorde, Cheryl Clarke, Sapphire, Cherrie Moraga, Gloria Anzaldua, or any of the female American Gladiators.

On lesbian dates, rarely does anyone discuss Jeff Stryker, River Phoenix, Ryan Idol, Kevin AuCoin, Ralph Lauren, Mel Gibson, David Geffen, Jean Claude Van Damme, Carl Lewis, the Pet Shop Boys, or any of the male American Gladiators.

Keanu Reeves, Drew Barrymore, Roseanne, Susie Bright, Bruce Bawer, and Michelangelo Signorile may be discussed during either date.

On gay men's dates, there may be sex even if neither party is very interested.

The likelihood that two women met on a phone sex line is slight.

The likelihood that two men met through a "Romance Only!" personal ad is slight.

Finally, the odds of men or women having met on-line is about equal.

**Q.** What's the future of lesbian dating?

**A.** As long as there are lesbians, I have to believe there will be lesbian dating. The only real change I see will be in the venues where these dates take place: virtual softball, satellite performance art; the possibilities are endless.

---

# THE DATING SCORECARD:

## The Beginning
▼ You actually both showed up and it was a blind date: +20
▼ You both showed up and you know each other:  +10

## During a Meal
▼ For each time you laughed together:  +5
▼ For each time one of you laughed and the other
  looked befuddled:  –5
▼ Each mention of one's own ex-girlfriend:  –5
▼ Each mention of the other's ex-girlfriend (the first
  two mentions are free, then):  –10
▼ Each awkward silence that wasn't broken within
  ten seconds:  –3
▼ Each time one of you said: "Exactly!," "Totally!," or
  "God, I love that!":  +2

## During an Event
▼ First time you accidentally brush against each other:  0
▼ Each time it happens "accidentally" after:  +3
▼ Whispering to each other:  +10
▼ Knees touching:  +5
  ▼ For more than a short period of time:  +15
▼ Hand holding:  +20
▼ Making out and missing most of it:
  ▼ If it wasn't out of boredom, or poor quality:  +150
  ▼ If it was:  0

## Afterward
▼ You go out for a drink:  +25
▼ You kiss goodnight:  +50
▼ More than once:  +25
▼ You go home together:  +250
  (but then it's not a date anymore, so you lose all your
  points.)

Kinky sex, for our purposes, is anything that you were taught was strange or unnatural, but turns you on. With this simple a definition, even the most "vanilla" lesbian sex becomes kinky. That's alright—there's an argument to be made for keeping it there.

What we're really discussing here, though, is that which is out of the range of the "typical" encounter between two women—those acts that are the most basic building blocks of sex. We're talking not far out of the orbit of the known, but far enough to make someone say "oooh, that sounds kind of fun."

Lesbian sexuality took a turn for the better, worse, or at least more discussed during "The Sex Wars." The symbolic moment pointed to as the shot heard round the world was the Barnard College Conference on Women and Sexuality (1983), where those who wanted to do workshops on such taboo subjects as S/M, butch/femme, and fantasy were soundly picketed (and later hounded) by women from the groups Women Against Violence Against Women and Women Against Pornography (WAVAM and WAP, respectively.) With the first shot fired, it would seem that all this pent-up energy exploded into dyke culture, with many detractors following at its heels. The end result, thirteen years later, has been numerous books on what women do in bed, from the cozy domesticity of *The Joy of Lesbian Sex* to Pat Califia's thorough and extensive non-fiction works on S/M and lesbian sexuality: *Sapphistry, The Lesbian S/M Handbook,* and *Sensuous Magic.* (In order not to reinvent the wheel here, you'll find a bibliography at the back of the book.)

The hardest thing about doing something new is that you don't know what you're doing until you practice. The hardest thing about doing something new sexually is getting past the feeling that you're doing something wrong, both mechanically and metaphysically. As mentioned in Lesbian Bed Death (see p. 70.), it's important to feel comfortable with what you're doing before you do it with someone else. (It doesn't mean you actually have to **know** what it is exactly, just that you won't pass out or run away when it happens.)

Discussed below are some of the more common "normal" and "kinky" things that make hearts beat a little faster.

## Bondage/Discipline (B/D)

It seems a safe bet that every relationship contains a small element of fantasy or experience with one or both of these.

Case in point: Wendy and Suzy are fooling around in the morning before going off to work. Suzy tickles Wendy and Wendy playfully tickles her back. Suzy does not enjoy being tickled and grabs Wendy's hands, placing them behind Wendy's back. Wendy struggles with her and Suzy tickles her mercilessly. They both fall back on the bed and have a morning jaunt before heading out to greet the world.

This playful, innocent romp would easily fall into the category of "light" B/D. Some women take this farther than others and invest in great amounts of hard- and software. We're not talking about computers here—ropes, chains, pulleys, scarves, and restraints will work much better that the 1995 edition of *Turbo Tax for MacIntosh*. If you're thinking something equipment-laden tickles your fancy, you might want to do some research. If garden-variety bondage is more your speed, common sense will suffice.

▼ Don't tie people up against their will. This isn't sex. It's violence.
▼ Leave enough space for fingers to fit, so circulation is maintained.
▼ If it's not fun, don't do it.

## Domination

Some women are simply more dominant or aggressive than others. Some enjoy being dominated in bed. Sometimes, these are the same women. Domination can either be the revenge of the dominated on her oppressors or else the natural overflowing of a person's nature. It can be a lot of fun making someone do things for you that she wants to do, but just needs the license of consensual "force" to let her enjoy it.

## Ménage à Trois:
## Or it's not just the two of us . . .

It's a concrete fact that you can be attracted to more than one person at any given time. Perhaps you and your partner might be attracted to the same person. One way to deal with this is to get extremely jealous and tag-team flirt with her until she comes onto one of you. The hit-upon declares herself the victor. Then you both forget about it, and compete about who's smarter.

Another way to handle it is for both of you to sleep with her. A three-way, or ménage, is a rather complicated process, yet has proven its interest to the human libido time and time again. If you're considering approaching this experience, a checklist might be in order:

▼ *"Do we both want to do this?"* You should be completely honest with each other. If one decides to do this to make the other woman happy, odds are it's going to suck and somebody's going to get hurt.

▼ *"Can we call it off?"* Make sure that you are both in agreement if one of you panics, or decides this isn't something she wants to pursue. If one of you will be *very* disappointed, perhaps you need to look at exactly what it was you were going to get out of this.

▼ *"Is the third woman amenable?"* Pretty much a yes or no question.

▼ *"Is there a term limit?"* As with Congress, a term limit can help prevent ugly entrenchment on an otherwise happy relationship. Everyone should understand the ground rules beforehand.

The more technical aspects, like what size bed is best, who gets to use the bathroom first, and whose house to go to are things best left up to the participants.

## Penetration

Most (but not all) women enjoy some form of this or another; some live by it, others have an infrequent but urgent need for it. If it's something you enjoy, you might want to explore other variations of what seems at first like a fairly straightforward process.

### Fisting

Good technical guides to this activity are (again) Pat Califia's books (sort of the godmother of kinky lesbian sex). Remember the basics:

▼ Trim your fingernails.

▼ Use lots of lubrication. A glove can also help, if lubricated, as well as preventing germs and things from being transmitted.

▼ STOP IF IT HURTS. As commonsensible as that sounds, you can forget in the heat of the moment. If there is any bleeding, stop immediately and make sure that it is nothing serious. If the bleeding hasn't stopped or if you think something is very wrong, get to a doctor or emergency room.

▼ Be patient. Rome wasn't built in a day, and forcing things will only cause pain and suffering.

## Dildos

These can really be anything from a handy vegetable to complex silicone implements in the shapes of endangered species. They all serve the same purpose however. Strap-on dildos can open up a whole new world of excitement, leave your hands free, allow more full body contact, and can be used in gender play. If you don't live in a large city, you might want to send for catalogues from Eve's Garden, Good Vibrations, and Babes in Toyland: These stores do mail-order catering to primarily women customers and have all kinds of goodies.

*Nota bene:* If you're going to use vegetables and plan to make a salad later, do not use lubricant.

## Anal Penetration

A book called *Anal Pleasure and Health* would be a good guide for those interested in the topic. You should practice all the precautions mentioned above for fisting with even greater vigilance, as the outcome is worse when you're not careful.

## Public Sex

This can either be the two of you, or in a group setting. Doing your girlfriend in the park or in a bathroom can be great fun. The only real danger is discovery; thus airports in foreign places are good (no blow to your reputation), your Aunt Edna's barn may not be.

# Role-Playing/Gender Fuck

Doctor and nurse. Librarian and patron. Nuns. We all have fantasies. Some are more elaborate than others, but everyone has a scenario in her mind that she'd like to make true someday. This is one kind of role-playing. Butch/femme is considered by some as role-playing, while others maintain that it's more essential, not unlike being gay/straight/bi. There are also those who like to take it one step further, passing as straight couples as a turn-on.

For playing out fantasies, communication is the most important part. Talking about your fantasies is a good way to see them come to fruition. "Oh honey, what a great birthday present! Three cheerleaders and a football uniform! You shouldn't have!" It's also a good way to make certain that it's something your partner would like to share. You wouldn't want to try and play out your conductor/cellist fantasy, only to find out that your girlfriend's dog was struck and killed by a crazed cellist at a tender age. This is certainly not an exhaustive guide. We don't pretend to know everything, and neither should anyone else. A wide variety of information is out there. You should feel free to pick and choose what makes you feel good.[1]

---

[1] Obligatory Mother Disclaimer: (who may be reading this book) Mom(s), we don't have first-hand experience (so to speak) with any of these things. Really. We swear. Really.

# MOVING IN TOGETHER

There comes a time in the youth of every relationship when questions rear their ugly heads: "Where are we going with this? Where do I see us in a year? Two years? Am I ready to make a more serious commitment to this woman? And does she feel the same way? Why is she always wearing my clothes?" And finally, "Should we move in together?"

This is a seemingly innocent and practical question, but beneath its simplicity lurks a number of issues that need to be addressed before either party can say with certainty that she's going into this with both eyes open. First ask yourself: "Why would we move in together?"

▼ *We're doing it because it will save us both money.*
>Obviously, saving money is a good reason. But if this is the main reason you're considering the move, read on.

▼ *We're doing it because we love each other.*
>This is a great reason to share a household (along with saving money). But have you examined the domestic issues that can drive two seemingly happy people to homicide: *"I can't fucking believe you left the cat food can on the counter again! How many times have I said . . . ?"* etc. Going on blind love and adoration can honestly only take you so far.

▼ *We're doing it to keep us together.*
>Simply put, this is a *bad reason. Bad bad bad.* Nothing will break you up faster than trying to salvage something that is having problems by intensifying it.

▼ *We're doing it because we're sick and tired of having to run home every morning to change clothes for work.*
>Fine, as long as that's not your primary motivation. Inconvenience is no reason to live with someone.

▼ *We're doing it because one of us really wanted to and the other felt really bad and didn't want to say no.*
     *Bad reason.*

▼ *We're doing it because one of us has this totally fabulous apartment and her roommate moved out, etc.*
     This could be either good or bad, depending on the other causative factors.

With this said, let's be phranc here: living together is not going to be a picnic every day of the year. There are bills to be paid, chores to be shared, pets to be dealt with, and the stress of living with someone who you can't just turn on and off like the hot water. Living with a roommate, you can always close your door or leave for a while if you're not quite up to being sociable. You can't just close your door on your lover. If you leave, she may think it's something she did. Unless you can communicate on a very honest level, living together can create an endless vicious cycle of hurt feelings, arguments, and not a little pain as you work out the personal quirks that you sometimes keep to yourself.

*But,* and this is a big but . . . living together can be ecstasy. Sharing space with someone can be one of the most truly splendid things about being with someone. It's like always having your best friend there to share things with, to cook with, to wake up with in a place that really is "yours." It's about coming home to someone you love every day, and having sex in the kitchen when you want to. Living together can truly bring you closer to someone you love.

If you can get through all of these warnings, and still decide that living together is for you, we hope the following will help you with the transition.

**Style:** By now, you should both have a decent idea of each other's living habits. If you've found yourselves bickering over things in this category, the best advice would be to sit down and talk about it before you're carrying each other over the threshold.

**Compromise:** Living with anyone requires a goodly amount of this. What compromise *doesn't* mean is "Okay, whatever you want." It does mean "How can we do this so we both feel like we have input?" So, if one of you simply can't bear the thought of washing dishes and the other feels like the next time she washes a dish, it's going to be in her own, spanking brand-new apartment, you need to sit down and figure out who's going to do what. Some couples divide these things up by room; "Okay, I'm in charge of the kitchen, you get the bathroom, we both get the living room and the bedroom, and your stinky dog is your problem." Some do it on a rotational schedule "Okay, I'll deal with the stinky dog three times a week, and you get him four."

This also works well when it comes to furniture. If you can't possibly live with her moosehead, and she won't get rid of it, you might figure out somewhere to keep it that won't offend your more delicate sensibilities. That's what storage facilities are for.

**Communication:** Again, you are lost without this. Whether it's about little things, like how annoying it is when the mail comes upstairs and disappears into this "black hole," or big things like how much your girlfriend's silent sulking is making you crazy, if you don't talk about it, it's going to get bigger and bigger until it finally comes out all wrong:

"Hi, honey, how was your day?"

"Fine, except that I couldn't register for school because it seems that my registration card came in the mail three weeks ago, and I never got it (seethe . . .)."

"Oops."

"That's it! . . . I'm outta here!"

**Tolerance:** There are just some things you can't change and shouldn't try to. If your girlfriend can't get up for work on time, no matter how many alarm clocks you set, you have to accept that. Remember, you're not her mother. She's an adult. Let her get herself up.

**Love:** Just because you're living together doesn't mean that you suddenly don't have to work at love anymore. If you want to keep the romance alive, pretend you're still dating sometimes. Get off the couch and go out with her. Bring her flowers. Leave notes around the house for her. In the immortal words of Winston Churchill, "Keep the home fires burning."

# ESSENTIAL KITCHEN GADGETS FOR THE WELL-STOCKED LESBIAN HOUSEHOLD:

▼ *Covered pyrex dish:* For potlucks, it's essential to have a good dish for your casserole.

▼ *Turkey baster:* For when the parents come on Thanksgiving, or for "alternative insemination," there's nothing that can beat a sturdy baster.

▼ *Rice steamer:* No macrobiotic should be without one.

▼ *Salad spinner:* Saves time on drying greens. Also good for emergency drying of underwear.

## Motorcycle Woman:

The biker girl comes in two basic varieties. Pictured is the butch version—with big boots, greasy hair and sneer that says, "Yeah that's right—I'm goin' in that ladies' room and you're not gonna stop me." She also exists in the femme variety, which is inclined towards bleached blonde hair, fringed leather jackets, and chaps. Care must be taken not to mistake her for Gloria Estefan during her Miami Sound Machine days.

# PMS²

## HOW TO SURVIVE SIMULTANEOUS MENSTRUATION

Is it an old wives' tale or proven scientific fact that women who spend a great deal of time together will synchronize their menstrual cycles? While we as Amazons and warriors welcome our monthly dance around the Maypole, it can lend itself to certain unpleasantries that come from the rise and fall of hormonal square dancing. Described below are some ways to deal with the Sturm und Drang of being a woman's woman when the old cycle of life comes a-callin'.

▼ *Keep separate supplies of everything necessary.*

If you're in a bad mood, and bleeding, the worst thing that can happen, the one thing that will send you out to buy a rocket launcher and cause massive carnage among your friends and family, is running out of "feminine sanitary protection." If you keep your own, apart from the other women in your life, you'll never be caught waddling out to the store with half a role of Charmin in your underwear to buy emergency supplies, and you'll have no one to blame but yourself if you do.

▼ *Learn your cycles and behave accordingly.*

Muffy and Bitzi are girlfriends. Muffy is on a twenty-eight day cycle and starting dropping dishes and crying at AT&T commercials three days before the onslaught. This lasts for forty-eight hours. Bitzi is on a thirty-day cycle, and gets very distraught about the tile grout four days before her womanhood. This lasts about thirty-six hours.

What can our usually happy-go-lucky women do to avoid an almost-certain household incident during their mutual menstrual difficulties?

▼ Remember, it's not you. It's your hormones talking.

▼ It's not the end of your relationship if your lover leaves the faucet dripping. There's more water falling on the earth everyday.

▼ Have a backup plan. Maybe staying at Kitzi's house during the worst of it isn't such a bad idea, as long as all of your boundary issues are in order (see Monogamy, p. 73).

Of course there are benefits to this phenomenon too.

▼ If you're menstruating together, then you're free and clear together too. Theoretically, if the women who are engaged in a mutual romantic endeavor don't have similar cycles, they could conceivably lose up to fourteen days of prime time together. This is often referred to as "The Antirhythm Method."

▼ For some women, their sexual desire becomes greatest for a few days before and a few days after their period. This gives the happy couple up to six days of mind-melting, sheet-ripping, "do-me-until-I-start-speaking-Sanskrit" sex without even having to work that hard for it. Then it's just the other twenty-two to twenty-five days you have to worry about.

# LESBIAN BED DEATH

## THE REAL STORY

Unless you've been ignoring the lesbian media for the past ten years, you're well acquainted with the phenomenon of Lesbian Bed Death (LBD). You're wondering "Am I doomed to linger in a sexless relationship forever if I hook up with someone for more than a week?[1] I had all these great fantasies of us actually living in the same house together . . . oh well, that one over there is cute. Hi, what's your name?" What is it that creates old nonwives' tales about how if you put a penny in a jar for every time women have sex in the first year together and then take one out every time they do it after that, the jar will never be empty? As with many phenomena in the community, a number of internal and societal factors are at play here:

### Socialization

While we've made great strides in overcoming women's socialization not to want sex "too much," we still carry those bags around with us.

Try some affirmations to overcome this aspect of our enslavement:

"I am not a slut. I am a powerful woman with an enormous lust for life." (Or maybe just "an enormous lust.")

"It is good and right that I want my girlfriend to plow me senseless every night."

"I am a beautiful woman who deserves to be worshipped in a black slip and stiletto heels."

Adapt these to your own preferences and repeat as necessary.

### Hooking Up with the Wrong People

It happens. We all make mistakes, some just last longer than others. A one-night stand becomes a three-year partnership. We're told as little girls that we need to truly love someone in order to go to bed with them. Or maybe we just get so infatuated with great sex that we overlook all of the other things that go into a good relationship. Or we over-

---

[1] Actual statistics place this closer to a year.

70

look the bad (or nonexistent) sex because we love them so much. Or we're codependent. We're all a mess, healing our inner children, doing our guided visualizations, doing our goddess work . . . whatever.

With the above in mind, here are the three secrets to having a Happy Lesbian Life:

▼ *It's okay to say no:* You can get out of an unhappy relationship. There's a whole world out there waiting for you once you're up to it. If being with someone is more painful than you think it should be, you probably need to look at what it is you're in this for. (If it hurts only occasionally, take a couple of Advil.)

▼ *It's okay to say yes:* It's absolutely right and good for you to have fun and not feel guilty about how much fun it is. It's good to take things lightly sometimes. Give yourself some license to be stupid.

▼ *Don't take any wooden nickels.*

## Bad Press from Straight People

Far be it from us to blame everything on straight people. But it wasn't us who wrote "two zeroes don't equal one" when discussing lesbianism. It was Dr. (and that term is used *very* loosely here) David Reuben, in *Everything You've Always Wanted to Know About Sex,* But Not About Anything Except Straight Sex because Dr. David Reuben is an *idiot.*

Of course, now that lesbians have made it into middle America's living rooms (and were probably in their bedrooms as well), we're beginning to be seen as the threat we'd like to think we all are. ("Hi, we're the homosexual menace. We've come for little Timmy.") So instead, they're hopping on the LBD bandwagon to take the wind out of sails and protect their wives and daughters.

"No, honey no. You'd don't want to go and be a dyke. Sure, it's good for a while, but with this bed-death thing, you'll be constantly prowling the alleys at night, looking for women in chaps to fulfill your raging desires."

## How to Prevent LBD

▼ *Mystery:* The element of surprise cannot be overestimated in its value. Making love at an unexpected place or time can add much to what may have become "You do this to me, I do this to you, did you lock the door, see you in the morning, zzzzzz."

▼ *Variety:* If you have already fallen into the above-mentioned pattern, vary your routine a little or a lot. Leave the shades up, wear something different. If you do it in silence, try using your vocal cords. If you're a Chatty Kathy, try to be silent (except for those more primal sounds you can't really control anyway). If you feel you've run the gamut of sexual expression, you're probably not thinking hard enough. Or you're Pat Califia.

Joann Loulan's books, *Lesbian Sex* and *Lesbian Passion* are two very good guides to sexuality between women (see Resource Guide, p. 221). If you've tried to enhance your sex life, and it seems there's something deeper going on, as there often may be, an outside source of support and advice might help. Therapy and counseling, clichéd as they are, can nevertheless help.

Unfortunately, as mentioned, sometimes the hardest conclusion is the right one: It has come time to end it. Frequently, if there are real problems in the relationship, they will manifest themselves in the bedroom. Either you're never making love or it's the only thing the two of you can stand to do together.

# MONOGAMY

HETEROSEXUAL SCOURGE
OR GENETIC PREDISPOSITION?

It has been argued by some geneticists that men are predetermined to cheat, a prehistoric urge to propagate the species and spread their genetic material far and wide; whereas a woman is predetermined to try and find one mate to take care of her and the products of the seed-spreading. Others may say that monogamy is a religious/economic conspiracy, created with a double standard firmly in place, where women were expected to remain faithful in marriage, having few rights and no property, while men could pretty much do what they wanted with little or no consequence.

In same-sex relationships without legal, societal, or even familial recognition, it seems that monogamy is something that has survived through the dogged persistence of those in the relationships. There are some in the gay and lesbian communities who make the arguments that monogamy is heterosexist and it is our hard-fought right and duty to love whomever and how many we want. While AIDS has certainly tamed the heady ethos of the 1970s for gay men, the 1980s seem to have been the clarion call of nonmonogamy in lesbian circles. The Sex Wars, depending on who you talk to, either brought about the destruction of sisterhood, or else was the liberation of our "dirty little secrets" (butch/femme, S/M, gender play).

Monogamy became one of the landmark issues in the debates. The freedom to sleep around without the benefit of a relationship (and all that implied) was a tenet of those declaring themselves "sex-positive."[1] However, some women who wanted to experience the joys of "no-strings attached" sex found obstacles strewn in the path to sexual freedom.

**1. Girlfriends:** No matter how enlightened she may be, it doesn't mean that your girlfriend will suddenly accept

---

[1] "Sex-positive" is used in this context in opposition to the antipornography, anti-S/M women who were referred to as "sex-negative" by the "sex-positive" women.

your need to sleep around. A lot of broken homes and animal-custody battles arose from this very issue.

2. **Themselves:** It was very hard to get past the feeling of unfaithfulness or the slut factor (no matter how encouraging the girlfriend).

3. **The community:** Being called a lech and a bimbo behind one's back (or to one's face) doesn't give those on the "barricades of the sexual revolution" much support.

Obviously, everyone has to find her own level of comfort. And screwing around because it's trendy doesn't mean you're happy doing it. Presented below is The Monogamy Index, for those who are interested in getting a handle (and an identifying number) on where they fall and a guide to others who may think similarly.

# The Monogamy Index

**0:** *Completely monogamous in both thought and deed.* There is no other in your eyes. Most nuns and those who have just fallen in love will be zeros (no value judgment implied).

**1:** *Completely monogamous in deed,* but . . . every once in a while, dreams of other women will creep into her consciousness. There may even be some flirting, but this is only testing one's attractiveness and a way of reminding herself that she still remembers how.

**2:** *Pretty monogamous in thought and deed.* Perhaps there have been a few slipups, at a drunken party—a kiss good-bye that went on a little long. Other than that, the couple rows merrily along.

With item 2, the issue of "Should I tell her?" begins to rear its ugly head. If this is a topic you've discussed in the past, then you'll know the answer to this question. If not, think before you speak. Think *hard.* Are you going to destroy something that means a great deal to you over a kiss? How do you think she will handle it? Is honesty something that outweighs the possibility of this demolishing your relationship? (As much as we'd like to tell you what to do, we don't carry that kind of malpractice insurance.)

**3:** *"Out-of-town" monogamy.* This is usually something practiced with the knowledge of both people. When the two women reside in the same city, they are monogamous. When one is out of town (business, family, etc.), both are free to pursue outside entertainment as long as it's not with anyone they both know and it is kept out of their relationship and it ends with the return of the traveling woman. Some people live very happy together this way. Then again, some people keep secrets better than others.

**4:** *Consensual nonmonogamy.* Both women agree that they are free to see other people within a set of agreed-upon stipulations. There are dangers in this however:

▼ *Jealousy:* Maybe Jenny wasn't really ready to watch Jill step out with a different woman every third night of the week. This can result in silent seething or outright drama.

▼ *Ambivalence:* Maybe Jenny actually gets out on her nights, while Jill sits home by the phone, hoping Jenny's date will cancel.

▼ *Love:* Maybe Jill meets someone who is so completely right for her that she decides her relationship with everyone else pales in comparison. Including Jenny.

These are all pitfalls that need to be thought about in advance before embarking on the experiment of free love.

**5:** *Nonconsensual nonmonogamy.* Traditionally referred to as cheating. Proceed at your own risk.

# SIX SIGNS YOUR GIRLFRIEND'S CHEATING:

▼ Her tattoo with your name on it has suddenly been changed into an abstract tribal band.

▼ She suddenly has voice mail, when a perfectly good answering machine was fine before

▼ She's working a lot of overtime at a new job that you didn't even know she applied for.

▼ She's wearing new underwear.

▼ She's suddenly going to visit her parents, whom she has not spoken to in ten years.

Finally,

▼ That big hickey on the side of her neck, that she insists was from walking into a door.

# GYNADDICTION

When Robin Norwood wrote her ground-breaking book, *Women Who Love Too Much,* she neglected a sizable portion of the market for her words of wisdom: Lesbians who don't know when to quit, who don't know when the line between "lover" and "servant" has been crossed, who can't say "no." The conditions of codependency between women are obviously different from those between members of straight couples: Firstly, there aren't many men to blame it on. This is sisterhood and sisterhood is powerful. Powerful enough to extinguish your ego completely and make you a sniveling pudding in the grip of a masterful woman who knows how to "work" you for everything you've got.

▼ *Women are raised as nurturers:* Whether or not one subscribes to a biological basis for this, we are taught to be caretakers. In a relationship between two caretakers this can take on a sick, twisted aspect of needing to coddle each other in infantilizing ways.

▼ *Women are expected to compensate:* The theory of compromise in relationships certainly wasn't suddenly thought up by some really sensitive guy.

▼ *Women are taught to try to make people happy:* If a woman does everything possible to avoid conflict, what are the chances that these conflicts will surface in a constructive way? About the same as the chances of you're being hit in the head by a parachuting Hillary Clinton wearing a gorilla suit, hawking health care.

With all this said, the conditions are ripe for painful, destructive relationships between loving, caring women who would ordinarily be perfectly happy with each other, until we meet that one woman who is looking for someone to solve all her problems, to become her mother and protector and feel everything for her, who turns her world upside down, and convinces her that life is nothing without them.

# I Think I'm Addicted to My Girlfriend:
## The *Cosmo* Test

How many lesbians go through their lives happy and content in healthy relationships that are mutually satisfying, long term, and allow for the retention of individual identities within the dyad?

It depends on who you talk to. Jesse Helms would probably say none. The National Lesbian and Gay Task Force would probably say hundreds of thousands. Individuals might say "I am the only one I know of." And other individuals would counter "Well, that's not really what I want anyway. I'm more into nonmonogamous sex dates right now." To which the National Lesbian and Gay Task Force would counter, "Yes, but heterosexual people do that, too. See, we really are just like everyone else. . . ." To which Jesse Helms would counter "But normal people don't use twenty-four-inch-long latex dildos to fulfill their twisted, perverted desires." At this point, someone would pipe in "Hey, Jesse, I don't know about you, but twenty-four inches seems like overkill." The conversation would degenerate into a cacophony of differing opinions, some valid, some political, and some wildly misinformed by some idiot's fantasy life.

Your girlfriend is in a snippy mood. A friend calls you to go out. You:

    A) think about it, and decide not to go because The Angels in Chains episode of "Charlie's Angels" is on tonight.

    B) welcome the opportunity to get away from Ms. "I've got a stick up my butt about something and I'm not going to tell you just to annoy you."

    C) decline gracefully, saying "I don't think it's such a hot idea. My girlfriend's in a bad mood."

You have just been offered a job at a social-service agency that both you and your girlfriend applied for. She wasn't even called for an interview. Now knowing this you:

    A) accept the job and try to deal with your girlfriend's feelings.

    B) accept the job and tell her to get over it.

    C) decline the position and try to convince the personnel director that she should really hire your girlfriend.

You have a problem with your mother. Your girlfriend asks you what's wrong. You say:

A) "Oh, my mom thinks that I'm stupid for not going to Ikea to get those bookshelves," which is the truth.

B) "Nothing," knowing it will blow over and it will work itself out.

C) "Oh sweetie, nothing is the matter when I'm with you."

Your girlfriend is going on a business trip. You:

A) kiss her good-bye and wish her good luck.

B) take her to the airport and watch the plane take off.

C) finagle a ticket to where she's going, hide out and watch movies in her hotel room all day, and then get depressed when she passes out from exhaustion at night.

Your family thinks maybe you've gone a bit overboard on this togetherness kick. You tell them:

A) "Hey, we'll grow out of it, we've only been going out for a couple of months."

B) "Oh, Mom, it's okay. I promise nothing surgical will happen."

C) "How can you do this? Why can't you support me in this? Just because we work in the same office, share an apartment, volunteer together, and are adopting together, it doesn't mean we don't have lives apart! It's not like we go to the bathroom together or anything! If I was straight, you'd be happy for me!!!"

You've started therapy. The first thing out of your mouth at the beginning of the session is:

A) "God, I'm so confused."

B) "God, my life sucks."

C) "God, my girlfriend is so depressed."

Your friends gather together and ask you to come. They've decided to do an intervention around your girlfriend addiction. You:

A) thank them profusely and see the light.

B) thank them profusely and flirt with the date of your first girlfriend from high school.

C) run screaming from the room, insisting they don't know what they're talking about, finally placing your hands over your ears, singing "I can't hear you, I can't hear you. . . ."

Your girlfriend leaves you, saying she can't take the pressure of being with someone whose entire happiness revolves around her. You:

A) cry for a little while, count your blessings, call all of your friends to commiserate, and go shopping for a new pair of motorcycle boots to cheer yourself up.

B) tear up all your pictures of her, burn her letters, and then go out, get drunk, and pick up a film student for comfort.

C) resolve to get her back, starting right now, calling her mother to ask her what you should do.

**Answers:**

A) Healthy constructive responses. Go get 'em killer.

B) This sounds more like an inability to commit.

C) *Run*, don't walk, to the nearest therapist (and not one for couples, either).

# DYKE DRAMA

In the film *Reality Bites* Janeane Garofalo tells Winona Ryder that "Love would be easier if I were a lesbian." Obviously, she has never been in a lesbian relationship, or she'd be familiar with the thing we call "dyke drama." Dyke drama takes on a variety of forms but mostly can be boiled down to two main categories—the benign "my life is a soap-operatic mess" strain where you as a girl's mate are continually brought into a never-ending series of bizarrely mundane problems that somehow manage to take on epic proportions or there is the "my girl-friend is an insensitive lout" variety where you as a girl's mate must deal with the ways that a woman can be unwittingly wicked to another woman. Here's a handy what-to-do-next guide in some prototypical dramatic scenarios that one may face as a woman-loving woman. Remember: Revenge is completely juvenile and potentially very satisfying.

1. *Scenario:* Girlfriend thinks she's a legend in her own time. She thinks every girl is hot for her and has a "little black book" of phone numbers bigger than Fonzie's on "Happy Days." Her main mode of communication is flirtation and she's always looking to score.

    *Counterscenario:* Remind her that life is not a beer commercial and every girl that talks to her is not in love with her. If all else fails, burn her "lucky" Hawaiian-print bowling shirt and take a baseball bat to her glow-in-the-dark Bud Light sign.

2. *Scenario:* Girlfriend is a windbag. She talks too much and is prone to long monologues even when answering the simplest question. This becomes especially annoying when she starts answering for others who are present.

    *Counterscenario:* As soon as she opens her mouth to talk, get up and leave to do something else. This is especially effective in a group situation. When girlfriend begins to hold forth, leave and take the entourage with you. Nothing speaks louder than a mass exodus. Then again, girl-friend probably won't even notice that they're gone.

3. *Scenario:* Girlfriend likes to make you the butt of jokes which are often about how a) frail b) weak c) stupid d) weird you are.

   *Counterscenario:* Pick a moment like when you have just purchased a large appliance that has to be delivered or brought into your house (a washer-dryer, refrigerator, or bed; a stereo system or color TV will do). Say in a sarcastic but helpless way "God, I'm so incompetent, can you help me with this?" Drop your end and let her struggle with it all by herself.

4. *Scenario:* Girlfriend is forever trying to find herself. She obsesses about what color to dye her hair, whether she's a Buddhist vegan punk or a nihilistic beatnik acid-jazz freak, a bike messenger or a poet, a paralegal or an art critic.

   *Counterscenario:* Flip her out by taking her to dinner at a steak house and demanding to sit in the smoking section even if you don't smoke, read a Camille Paglia book in her presence, go to Mass, wear an all leather outfit, and refuse to sort your recyclables.

5. *Scenario:* Girlfriend is totally self-obsessed and all she ever talks or thinks about is me, me, me.

   *Counterscenario:* This is easy, because if she is truly self-involved, she's probably in therapy (or, if you are really unlucky, a twelve-step program). There exists a special rule for confronting people in therapy—you don't have to be nice to them, you can tell them that you're tired of their self-obsessions or whatever else it is that bothers you about them. You needn't spare anyone's feelings because no matter how upset she may get, she can always talk it out with her therapist next week.

**6.** *Scenario:* Walking down the street, you and your girl pass a tall, leggy blond with fake-and-bake bronzed skin and 36DDDD siliconed tits. Your girlfriend drools.

*Counterscenario:* "Accidentally" throw out her Miss October, Farrah Fawcett, and St. Pauli Girl pinups.

**7.** *Scenario:* Whether by invention or by bad luck, girl-friend rivals Tonya Harding in the "I have a problem" department. Between you and her there is always some huge, overburdening problem that she must discuss end-lessly, not of course until it is resolved, but until some other huge predicament comes along. You've heard one too many stories about how she left her wallet at the de-partment store and her car was towed but she didn't have any ID or a cash card to get it back and could you come get her.

*Counterscenario:* Wait until girlfriend obsesses over some relatively minor problem and then say you think *that* is bad and launch into some humongous tirade about your chain-reaction bad day. If she tries to top it with another story, make up an even worse one. Con-tinue until one (or both) of you implode.

**8.** *Scenario:* You come to realize that your girlfriend is a chronic liar. She has an excuse for everything.

*Counterscenario:* Catching her in her lies can be great fun. Learn to lie yourself. It might lead to a whole new career as a fiction writer. When a friend tells you your girlfriend is two-timing you with an exotic dancer from the Kit Kat Klub named Bunny, begin the dinner conver-sation by saying, "Did I tell you I got a job to make some extra cash? Yeah, it's at the Kit Kat Klub. I'm a go-go dancer."

No relationship is ever perfect, but the soaring highs and the abysmal lows of life with a drama queen can be quite rewarding as long as one stays on one's toes. What fun is a peaceful and sedate union when you can rant and rave like a lunatic and still feel comparatively sane? Actually, the best part about dyke drama is when, after the fighting, the screaming, the crying, the clothes shredding, the dish smashing, and the car crashing, you make up (and you almost always do, at least once) with ten times the intensity of the fighting. Sometimes it is even worth fighting just to lie in your girlfriend's arms *après* a night of making up. Ooops, that would be Number 9—girls who start fights just to make up.

# QUICK WAYS TO DEFUSE DYKE DRAMA:

▼ *Cold Water:* If applied quickly and judiciously to the hysterical party, it can calm her down, as well as reduce dehydration due to overexertion.

▼ *Fire Extinguisher:* While not ideal, can be used to deflect attention long enough for a quick getaway or for a third party to step in.

▼ *Raw Meat:* Aside from the novelty factor, using a raw steak (not ground meat) to slap or hit the hysterical party can often bring her around to the absurdity of her behavior, e. g. "Wow, I must be really out of control. You just hit me with a porterhouse."

▼ *Weebles:* The comforting effect of watching Weebles (which wobble, but do not fall down unless you really hurt them) can help break the tension in a difficult situation. Also, if things get out of hand and you're forced to defend yourself, you can throw them with a goodly amount of accuracy.

# BREAKING UP IS
# HARD TO DO

Now you have mastered the odds, successfully coupled, and it is time to call it quits. Setting off on your own separate way can be very difficult and painful indeed. In general, when it comes to breaking up, there are only two positions in respect to the cold corpse of your formerly loving relationship: those who feel they have been fucked over and those who do the fucking over. The unique thing about these two sides, unless your ex-mate is Amanda Woodward on "Melrose Place," is that each person believes that she is the one who is being fucked over. This makes breaking up really hard work. But a painful breakup is a face-saving measure designed to ease you through your nostalgia for the good times by making you ponder what you ever saw in such a moron. It also gives you a way to rebond with your friends who you neglected all those years, months, weeks you were with your girlfriend by allowing them to act superior because they tried to tell you she was a jerk but you wouldn't listen. Here's a handy guide to what to do in the many horrific situations which result from love lost:

## Moving Out

Lesbians, by virtue of their less robust economic situation, tend to move in together to save money, to offer someone a place to live, or out of some other humanitarian reason. However, when everything is settled and boring and the itch to play the field comes back, the realization that the humanitarian gesture was also just a commitment disguised as goodwill becomes frighteningly evident (see Moving in Together, p. 64).

It is unrealistic to expect that you can just tell someone to get lost and she leaves. Moving out takes time. Whoever leaves, whether you or your girlfriend, will need time to find somewhere to go or make arrangements to acquire another abode. Therefore, it is best to remain calm and rational and talk about the impending "divorce" and discuss how much time it will take before the designated leave taker can find a place to go. Try to set a target date so that the one who stays can either make arrangements for another subletter, or roommate to take her place.

It is not unreasonable to set up ground rules for the time when you are still stuck together, perhaps, unamicably. The temptation may be to either try to rekindle the romance or get licks in at one another before you split. Either one of these does not lend itself to a happy or healthy home, therefore, deciding that one of you should sleep on the couch or another room is not the unkind cut it may at first seem. Finally, agreeing that neither one of you will bring someone else home is probably smart too.

## Who Leaves and Who Stays

The one who moves out should be the one who moved in last. If it was your place first, you stay, she leaves. (If you own the house or apartment jointly, go directly to the section on "Lawyers.") This seems obvious, but it is easier said than done. No one ever leaves without a hassle. If you are the one who wants to break it off and it is your abode, it may be hard to tell someone that you don't want to be with her and are kicking her out. Rarely is this received well either. A number of really bad things that could happen: She could decide that she hates you so much that she runs off leaving all her stuff behind. She could decide that she hates you, but she doesn't want you to be happy, so she will hang around forever, never planning to leave, or she could handle it fine and just look for her own place and move out with no problem. Experience has shown that the last is not likely.

Some people have a knack for handling the "my girlfriend won't leave" trauma with flair. For instance, there is one mythic story that has circulated about a particularly bad breakup. The girl whose house it was asked her girlfriend to move in with her, but after a number of months, found out that her girlfriend had continued to carry on a number of outside affairs and broke off the relationship. She requested that her now ex-girl look for a new place to stay, but the girl just disappeared, leaving all her stuff at her ex-girl's house. A few weeks later, she then showed up and begged to stay because she needed a place to crash. She did this several more times until the girlfriend tired of her ex-girlfriend's junk and periodic returns. The party of the first part packed up all the ex-girlfriend's stuff while she was out fooling around and sent it to her ex-girlfriend's best friend in another city. When the ex-girlfriend finally came back, all she found was a note explaining where her stuff was and a one-way airplane ticket to get it. We hope, you will not have to resort to this, but keep it in mind, just in case.

If you decide you want out, it may be best to make alternate living arrangements before telling the girlfriend that you want to leave/break up. However, if the girlfriend left behind needs to take on a roommate/housemate to pay bills, at least one month's notice is polite. This presents somewhat of a problem. You will want to avoid the unpleasant situation of living with someone who, once they find out that you are leaving/breaking up, will simultaneously hate/resent and love/desire you. Sometimes even the best laid plans backfire and the girlfriend may find out you are planning your escape and will confront you. If this happens it may be better to stay away from your shared place of residence for a while. Consider staying with a friend or family until you have another place to call your own. Otherwise, temporarily sublet your share of the *grand palais* to a friend or friend of a friend while you stay elsewhere and look for a *grand palais* of your own. No matter what, going back to the hellhole may not be the best thing to do right away.

## Money

A friend once told me about what happened when she lent her girlfriend money and they subsequently broke up with the ex-girlfriend still in debt to my friend. This cautionary tale should illustrate why one should never be a creditor of one's ex.

*The tale:* A few weeks after my friend's ex moved out and still owed her almost three months back rent and utilities, my friend ran into her at a restaurant. The ex-girl was wearing a full-length, real-fur coat. When my friend asked her about it, the ex told her that her new girlfriend just gave it to her. My friend was seething. She could sell the coat and pay my friend back and still have enough left to feed all of Haiti for at least a year. She longed for some blood to throw, not for political reasons but out of blind, raging anger. She never meant to get sucked in and lend the girl any money, but little by little it all added up. When they broke up, the girl couldn't pay her back. My friend tried to talk to her ex-girlfriend about the money but when she did, her girlfriend accused her of being petty.

*The moral:* If you have not received payment by the time your re-

## James Dean Wannabee:

A forever-icon in dykonology, James Dean has inspired more lesbians to wear white T-shirts, experiment with hair goop, and cut their hair short than any of the many adolescent sensitive male types. While a precision lookalike will go out of her way for the red windbreaker, proper khakis, curled lip, and wounded look, pretty much anyone can try this one. A prime example of the democratic nature of lesbian fashion.

lationship ends, you can kiss your bucks good-bye. Any attempts to collect money that is owed to you post-breakup will be greeted with hostility no matter who dumped whom. If you were dumped, she will see it as your way of getting revenge and if you dumped her, she will see it as you just trying to fuck her over once again. If caught in this situation, one should not rule out the possibility of hiring a collection agency to nag her for repayment.

While the problems of separating joint financial enterprises are beyond the scope of this book (since our idea of a joint checking account is sharing a jar of pennies to be rolled), it is safe to say you should definitely consult a lawyer if there is shared property or finances. If you have these things, you probably know this already.

## Clothing/Books/Records

This may verge on the realm of the petty, but one often forms profound attachments to certain items of clothing or whatnot. Should a selfish ex-girlfriend attempt to "acquire" your favorite Cultural Studies Reader or your soundtrack to the *Valley of the Dolls* in the moving-out process, you have every right to hire the bouncer at the local dyke bar to get them back by force. The real Golden Rule should be: You have the right to leave a relationship owning the exact same things that you did going into it.

## Gifts

When a relationship ends it is only polite to offer to return expensive gifts like jewelry, rings, etc. This means that it is okay to keep the Ron Popeil pasta maker and cubic zirconium ring your girlfriend bought from Suzanne Sommers on QVC, but one should at least offer to return the VCR and the Jil Sanders suit.

If you were lucky enough to receive joint presents from friends for your anniversary or housewarming, these may be divided between the two of you. Or you can donate them to charity. Or you can slowly hock them before the final breakup and play ignorant when girlfriend asks "Whatever happened to the salad spinner?"

# Pets

Should you have joint pets and both of you want to keep the pet, the best way to figure out who should take custody is to ask the pet which person it prefers. You do this by putting the pet alone in a closed-off room, later both of you walk in and the person that the pet greets the longest is the one it likes most and is thus now the new single owner of the pet. (Should you particularly desire the pet, carry food in your pocket or rub your hands with some type of meat or fish.)

## Breaking Up When You Are Not Living Together

1. Adopt what Miss Manners calls the Kafka approach. Don't call her or if she calls you, don't return her calls. Miss Manners believes that eventually she will get the message and leave you alone. She also points out that the advantage of this rather draconian approach is that you do not have to go through an embarrassing and painful conversation where you enumerate the shortcomings that have caused your breakup. (If only people really disappeared when you don't call them back, she might have something.)

2. If you were dumped or if you are trying to dump her, but find yourself wanting to call her against your better judgment, do something to take your mind off talking to her. Go to a movie, a museum, a mall, call another friend, get out of the house, but go somewhere new or somewhere that you love. DO NOT go anywhere that you went together as this will only aggravate feelings of nostalgia.

3. Distract yourself from obsessing about her constantly. It is not good to think about someone for more than $\frac{1}{2}$ of a whole day. If you find that you have exceeded the allotted time, take up a new hobby, join a new group, take an aerobics class.

4. If you must obsess, do something constructive with your obsession. Get revenge. Write a novel, join a band and

write all your lyrics about what an ass your ex is. Do it well enough and you can laugh all the way to the bank.

5. Rebounding.
*Con:* Tempting though it is, it just creates a whole new set of problems to deal with and it is totally un-pc.
*Pro:* It's nice to have new problems when old ones are draining you. In pursuing a girl with revenge potential, you need someone who is either smarter, funnier, wealthier, or better looking than your ex. Then you need to make sure your mutual friends meet her so that your ex will hear all about her.

## Dysfunctional Methods of Breaking Up That Are Best Avoided

1. Do not send a letter announcing your intention to break up with your girl via Federal Express.

2. Do not break up via e-mail unless the relationship was only an electronic one.

3. Do not decide to break up with someone and not bother telling her but start dating new people anyway. It is inevitable that the new girl you have just started to date is your not-yet-ex-girlfriend's best friend's ex-girlfriend, old girlfriend of your not-yet-ex's best friend's best friend, or something that will end up with your soon-to-be ex being the first one in the whole fucking world to hear about who you just spent the night with.

4. Do not serve your girlfriend with papers for your palimony suit before you have told her that you have broken up with her.

5. Do not hire a hit man or woman to take your girlfriend out. (No matter how tempting!)

# Breakup Songs to Ease the Pain

"A Woman Left Lonely"—Janis Joplin

"Three Cigarettes (in an Ashtray)"—Patsy Cline

"You're So Vain"—Carly Simon

"Manipulate"—Tribe 8

"Demirep"—Bikini Kill

"Bruise Violet"—Babes in Toyland

"Violet" or "Babydoll"—Hole

# The VH-1 Guide to Breakup Music for People who actually like Sting

"Fragile"—Sting

"Don't Want to Lose You"—Gloria Estefan

"Missing"—Everything But The Girl (They're actually good, don't be fooled by their inclusion on this list)

"Hold Me Now"—Thompson Twins

"Crazy For You"—Modonna

"Stay Free"—The Clash

# Culture

# AN INTRODUCTION TO LESBIAN CULTURE

What is Lesbian Culture? There is no simple answer to this question, because contrary to popular opinion, there really is no single "culture."

Nevertheless, there are four elements to any particular article that can be included under the umbrella term of "lesbian culture."

1. **Economy:** Dykes like more bang for their buck. So whether it's food, shoes, or vehicles, for the most part, you'll find girls getting things which are a good deal.

2. **Practicality:** If you can't use it, it's not worth having. Rarely will you find a lesbian household filled with useless *tchotchkes*. Even the most unassuming knickknack probably has a hidden can opener.

3. **Style:** The prevailing aesthetic is slightly skewed toward butch, but nonetheless is a unique and funky one for all involved. Really, who else would have started wearing gas station jackets and knit caps, if West Coast lesbians hadn't started it?

4. **Threat:** There is always a slight edge of danger in lesbian culture: the danger of discovery, the danger of desire, the danger of having your ex-girlfriend in the audience at your concert where all you do is sing about what a bitch she was to you while you lived together. Lesbian culture is all about living dangerously. With this in mind, read on and learn everything you need to know about dykes and their pop affections.

# GREAT CONTRIBUTIONS TO POPULAR CULTURE MADE BY LESBIANS

▼ **Backpacks:** Sure, now everyone's got one, but who was wearing them first? Whether for environmental reasons, or economic, or the obsessive-compulsive need to carry your entire life on your back (you can't very well fight patriarchy without the proper equipment) lesbians made these functional tools of existence into millions of dollars a year for the fashion and sporting goods industries.

▼ **Individually wrapped feminine products:** Since a good number of lesbians don't carry purses (and who wants to lug their entire backpack to the women's room), the demand for a pad you can put in your jeans pocket created these helpful, prewrapped napkins. (Tampons already had their own wrapping. However, if you were *really* butch, you just stuck your Stayfree in your back pocket and proudly strutted to the facilities.) Unfortunately a new debate has developed: non-biodegradable wrappers.

▼ **Public toplessness:** Having come home from various women's music festivals, empowered by the freedom of going *au naturel* among thousands of like-minded women, the girls began to fight for the right to do the same at home. While only a handful (so to speak) take advantage, the rest of us are the better for it, if only to piss off public officials.

▼ **Wash and Wear Haircuts:** (see The Great Lesbian Haircut Conspiracy, p. 102).

▼ **Porn for women, by women:** A great leap in sexual liberation or just buying into the exploitation of our sisters? Whatever your position, it's at least more satisfying than watching two surgically enhanced types "get it on" with unreal fingernails (hello? ouch!) and then have some guy "accidentally" walk in on them and take over.

▼ **Appreciation of non-European cuisine by those not born to it:** (see Lesbian Cuisine, p. 104).

▼ **Librarian worship:** (see Real World Role Models, p. 178.)

# CLOTHING AND FASHION

## THEY'RE NOT THE SAME THING

Lesbians have gotten a bad rap for hundreds of years (okay, at least forty or so) when it comes to fashion. Accused of everything from bad haircuts (see below) to dressing like men, they have borne the brunt of a closed-minded cultural imperative of "femininity," "good taste," and the fears of those who would have you believe that the underlying politics of being a dyke are to get all the women of the world to stop shaving their legs and underarms and start raiding the closets (so to speak) of the male powers-that-be. But ask yourself this—have you ever seen a lesbian in a lime green leisure suit? We think not.

Now that "lesbian chic" has hit big, people have suddenly decided that dykes are cool and know what they're doing. We knew that all along. It always takes straight America years to catch up (like who discovered Calvin Kleins first, huh?). Let's examine the basic building blocks of lesbian style: the must-haves, the "little extras," and of course, the big fashion no-nos that no matter what team you're playing on at the moment, you shouldn't even think about putting on your body.

## Must-Haves

1. **Leather jacket.** It doesn't have to be a motorcycle jacket—as long as it's black. Some people shy away from leather for fear that it will communicate an adherence to a strict sexual philosophy that implies a lot of cold, metal apparatus and a bandanna code that you actually need a book to figure out. Rest assured—most people who wear it don't have a clue as to what a navy hankie in your right pocket means (but if you do, go for it, girl). What leather communicates is the essential animal nature in all of us: "Sure, we can write symphonies and paint and think about gravity, but we still have needs."

    Favored models are: welder's jackets—three-quarter

length, big pockets, preferably well broken in; bomber jackets—these fall in and out of favor, but if worn properly are quite the look; police jackets—these bring the added bonus (or problem) of attracting women with a uniform fetish; and yes, the motorcycle jacket—always a little dangerous, can go either way (girly or not), can be worn with anything, and will get better with age.

2. **Big, Black, Clunky Shoes.** When in doubt about a woman's predilections, a glance at her feet will often steer you in the right direction. These can be boots (the almost-too-cool pole-climbers, Dr. Martens, combat boots, "engineer" boots, or any variation of these) or shoes (Docs again, Georgia shoes, police oxfords). Sandals don't cut it, no matter how big they are. The history of the big, clunky, black shoe has yet to be written, but probably intersects with the all-encompassing EPST rule of queer fashion as a whole: *Economy, Practicality, Style,* and *Threat.*

3. **Levi's 501s.** Need more be said. Their message of casual, up-front sexiness that has captured the minds, hearts, and libidos of America was first hit upon by gay men and has made Levi-Strauss a bundle. Worn full length or cut off, many women have discovered their attraction to the same sex while playing with the buttons on their "best friend's" jeans.

   *A note of caution:* If worn too tight, instead of saying "Hi there . . .," you may find your pants screaming "I'm a bimbo. Don't come near me if you have a brain in your head."

4. **Boxer Shorts.** No, no one is encouraging you to cross-dress. The same aesthetic that makes men's dress shirts sexy, works for their big underwear, too—there's something uncommonly attractive about a woman in a pair of oversized, plaid (or plain or striped or print) boxers. They can be worn underneath your clothes (hence the term underwear, but you knew that) or as shorts. If you choose this summer casual look, one need not be reminded that you might want to keep your Jockey for Her around in these instances—no one wants to be walking around with her pudenda hanging out.

5. **T-shirts.** It's been said that if there were no lesbians, there would be a lot fewer T-shirts in the world. Again the EPST rule applies here. Most-favored T-shirt status goes to: plain white undershirts (crew neck, V neck, or tank), kooky retail store/promotional shirts from obscure towns ("Twelfth Annual Flounder Toss—King's Point, Nebraska"), anything Harley-Davidson, and of course, various activist shirts. Cutting the sleeves off is optional, and if it's going to get cold where you are, just think about trying to sew them all back on.

## Accessories You Should Consider

1. **Trucker Wallet.** As one always needs a place for the effluvia of everyday life, you can't go wrong if it's basic black. There are plain wallets, ones with various seventies TV characters, and the new "designer" wallets, all acceptable. The chain can be clipped to your belt or belt loop, thereby achieving a certain grunge/skate kid panache, or in more formal times, you can carry the wallet like a clutch. You'll never lose it in those more intimate moments, and there's even an attachment for your keys (this, however, tends to stray into a janitorial fetish that we just don't know enough about to advise you).

2. **Tattoos.** Everybody's doing it (or so you'd think). Here are the important issues to consider:
   *Permanence:* Sure you can get them removed, but they're not cheap in the first place and it costs at least four times as much to get rid of them. Think long and hard about **what** you're going to get and where it's going. (Will you be doomed to wear full body makeup to family reunions and just how long is this relationship going to last? Remember Johnny Depp. Winona was NOT 4-ever.)
   *Pain:* One recently tattooed chick said this: "It didn't hurt enough to make me scream or anything. It did make me whine a lot, though." The experience is not unlike someone scraping the area with a blunt butter knife. Different body parts hurt unequally—the less fleshy or sensitive, the more you're going to feel it.

*Design:* As mentioned above, not to be taken lightly. The bigger, the more expensive, the more pain. A good rule of thumb from a tattoo artist: "Start small. You can always get more." If you're not out at your job/to your family/at the convent, you might want to skip that "I ♥ PUSSY" tattoo right now.

3. **Baseball caps.** For fashion, bad hair day/month/year (see below) or to actually support a hometown team, you can't go wrong.

4. **Oval-frame glasses.** Sometime around 1993, these exploded, and everyone started looking like a Russian intellectual. If you don't have to wear regular glasses, the sunglass version is just as fetching. Invest in a sturdy pair if you have a tendency to sit on them.

5. **A cocktail dress.** It's a good bet that at least once in your life, someone is going to give a dress-up party that you're invited to. Rather than wearing the same old thing, or sitting at home moping, go to all the used-clothing/garage sales you have to until you find that one perfect frock. It will serve you well, and let people know you have a kicky, playful side that might be hard to find under the leather jacket. (If you'd rather die than wear a dress, then consider a good suit.)

## Do Not Wear These—Ever

1. **Ponchos.** Unless they are crushed velvet and worn with black leggings, the only people wearing ponchos should be residing in places where Quetzalcoatl was worshipped. Or still are bummed out that the Dead are, in fact, dead.

2. **Cowboy boots.** These are very over in the urban United States. However, if you punch cows for a living, please ignore this.

3. **Western shirts.** Ditto. If you happen to be wearing both the shirt and boots in a performance art tribute to k. d lang: the early years, go right ahead.

4. **Men's golfing clothes.** There's not even anything re-deemably campy about them. *Nobody* looks good in these.

5. **Flannel without irony.** The grunge years brought flannel back with a vengeance, but the contentious rela-tionship between lesbians and plaid flannel shirts has yet to be overcome. Cutting the sleeves off helps. Being seventeen helps more.

## The Great Lesbian Haircut Conspiracy

Perhaps no one thing has plagued the Sapphic sisters more (aside from invisibility, violence, and homophobia) than the Bad Haircut Conspir-acy. For years, people have accused lesbians of deliberately setting out to get bad haircuts, thereby destroying the moral fabric of society (how, we'll never know). But years of research has finally answered the question of why you can't get a decent haircut no matter where you go.

### Paris, 1927:

Gertrude Stein and Alice B. Toklas have become great good friends with Ernest Hemingway. Little do they know that Ernest has been bad-mouthing them all over the city, to anyone and everyone who would lis-ten (there are hints of Gertrude's seducing one of Ernest's wives with Alice's brownies). One day, when Gertie and Alice go to have their meticulous coiffures done, they discover in horror their hairdresser has fled the city in fear, due to a bad perm that has earned the ire and scorn of the entire *arrondisement*. Hearing their tale of woe, Ernest recom-mends his personal barber, Jean-Luc "Bud" Bouville, who does the entire Hemingway family. They thank Ernest profusely and hasten on their way.

Ernest calls ahead, and asks Bud to join him in a little practical joke—would he shave the heads of the two women who he has just sent over? Bud, always up for a good laugh, agrees, and as Gertrude settles herself in the barber's chair, he leads her like a lamb to the shearing. Alice is shorn likewise.

They both return home, feeling light as a feather, thrilled with their new and daring dos. They recommend Bud to everyone, and soon the entire Sapphic demimonde is besieging Bud with requests for ap-pointments. Ernest is furious, thinking that Gertrude is too stupid to know an insult when she sees it and vows to get even with that "cow" some-day when she can't return fire. He fulfills this vow in *A Moveable Feast*.

Meanwhile, Bud submits an article on "Inverts and Hairdressing" to *Hair Quarterly*, discussing his newfound clientele and in doing so dooms an entire segment of the female population to his misguided, psychobabble hairdressing theories, which are clung to like gospel by fellow barbers.

# LESBIAN CUISINE

OR
BEYOND GRANOLA AND BACK AGAIN

One of the many ways that lesbians express their dissatisfaction with the world in which they live is by turning against the basic structures that reinforce capitalism, patriarchy, heterosexual privilege, Newt Gingrich, etc. One very important facet of this rebellion against mainstream society is the modern lesbian formation of an alternative gastronomy. Or in other words, dykes who don't wear dresses certainly aren't going to eat just any old burger and hot dog. What follows is a handy guide to lesbian cuisine for those who want to be dykes or even just eat like one.

## International

In an effort to exhibit their multicultural prowess, lesbians feel that ethnic foods are a must. Every lesbian knows at least two hundred ways to serve tahini. A quick peek in any dyke cupboard will reveal boxes and boxes of couscous, the Moroccan pasta. When dining out, even the most most affluent lesbian favors the inexpensive and scrumptious cuisines of such famine-plagued lands as India, Ethiopia, Thailand, and the Caribbean.

## Of Edensoy and Soba Noodles

Many lesbians also favor the so-called macrobiotic foods easily mistaken for compost. Topping the edible organic matter lists are: kefir, carob, bulgur, hijiki, and the many soybean products (see below).

## Tofu

Tofu is a waterproof, spongy white food made from coagulated soy milk. It is high in protein, calcium, and other nutrients but the trade-off is its complete lack of flavor. As Velveeta is to the rest of the country, tofu is to the lesbian: A universal basic with a myriad of culinary uses. Witness just a few, tofu pups (as opposed to hot dogs), tofu burgers, tofu lasagna, and for dessert, tofu flan. Hey it's more than a bean, it's a lifestyle.

## A Vegan, Two Thousand Vegetarians, and a Dinner Party

The first rule of thumb for those interested in entertaining lesbians—do not serve meat. It's not just that a good number of lesbians are vegetarians it's that they are lacto-vegetarians, lacto-ovo-vegetarians, pesco-vegetarians, and pollo-vegetarians. Then there are vegans, who for ethical reasons, decide not to support the cattle or poultry industries on the grounds that they are cruel to animals. Vegans are haunted by the idea of the poor hen who continually lays her eggs only to have each little chicken-to-be continually snatched out from under her. Thus, no animal flesh will touch a vegan's lips. Nor do vegans wear clothes which have been made with animal skins or products. When there's more than one dyke at a meal, it's a wonder if anyone ever eats more than peanut butter and jelly.

## Beer

The cruelty-free beverage of choice for all lesbians. It seems no one cares about the lowly hop.

## Ho-Hos, Ding Dongs, and Sno Balls

Some lesbians choose to eat food cruel to neither animal, vegetable, nor mineral and ingest only preservatives. Thus they are cruel to only themselves. In the throes of a mad sugar rush, junk-food addicts have been known to murder vegans when lectured about the hazards of their habits.

## Stir-fry

It doesn't matter what you put in it, Ho-Hos, Twinkies, a Big Mac, just add tofu and stir fry. If it's stir-fried everyone will be happy!

## Granola

Yes, it's a cliché, but it's true. Some lesbians have even been spotted making their own.

## Big Sloppy Heroes

No one quite understands why, but many the lesbian is known to sneak down to the local sub place and indulge, particularly butch women. We're not one to draw conclusions, but sometimes a submarine sandwich may be a lesbian phallus.

## Herbal Tea

From Sleepytime to Lemon Zinger, lesbians are the only group of people truly well acquainted with the wide variety of decaffeinated teas. If lesbians didn't exist, neither would Celestial Seasonings.

## Potluck

Combine all the elements above (save the junk food), add a Cris Williamson tape, and shake well.

# FAVORITE LESBIAN VEHICLES

**Motorcycles** of any make or model: Deep down inside every lesbian truly yearns to be a dyke on a bike.

**Thunderbirds** (vintage): Thelma and Louise drove one. All "bad" women drive Thunderbirds.

**Trans Am:** Because guys aren't the only ones who like to blare Led Zeppelin and cruise mall parking lots looking for chicks.

**pickups** or four-wheel drive vehicles: For butch lesbians who feel that every vehicle should be first and foremost a utility vehicle.

**Mazda Miata:** The femme vehicle of choice, because only femmes believe that the sole purpose of a vehicle is to make you look good. Should a femme need a utility vehicle, she just calls one of her butch friends.

**Volvo wagons:** Change a few letters and the name says it all.

**Saabs:** A sort of counterculture BMW. A status symbol for lesbians with a steady job and a healthy cash flow. Perhaps it is the odd slightly egg-shaped design that lesbians find comforting. *Alternate:* For those lesbians without the pocketbook for an import, try the AMC Pacer (aka "The Bubble Car").

**public transportation:** Not because you don't own a car, but because you want to conserve energy.

**unicycle:** A favorite at wimmin's festivals and arts-and-crafts fairs. Usually found next to mimes.

**collapsible bicycle:** The ultimate triumph of function over form, so you know it was probably invented by a lesbian.

## Jock Girl:

This type is relentless in her pursuit of two things: a good pick-up softball game and the opportunity to beat opponents senseless (metaphorically speaking—most of the time). Always looking for a chance to play something—it may be difficult to get her to think about anything else. You might try playing "Flag Football" in the bedroom, or racing her to the local sex toy shop. Once she's winded enough, you might get her to pay attention.

# I WANT TO GO WHERE THE GIRLS ARE: A QUICK GUIDE TO LIVING AND LEARNING WITH OTHER LESBIANS

## Geography

Suppose you have just realized that you are a dyke. Now you are faced with the dilemma, "Where do I go to be where the dykes are?" Well, furrow that brow no more, here's a quick guide to the major cosmopolitan areas with large dyke populations. For the purpose of housing, the lesbian community can be divided up into two camps—the crunchy and the grouchy. The crunchy live perfect, collective lives in sunny peace and harmony, while the grouchy eke out a bitter and meager existence in nihilistic exile from the crunchies. To decide if you are a crunchy or a grouchy take this quick diagnostic test:

When I hear the words, "Tomorrow, tomorrow, I love ya tomorrow." My next response is—

    A.  I smile and tell the first person I see that I had a crush on Andrea McArdle, the girl who played Annie.
    B.  I want to bang my head against the wall until the ringing in my ears is so loud that I can't hear anything let alone that song!

It should be fairly obvious that if you answered "A," well then you can go with crunchies and if you picked "B," well then you need intense psychiatric counseling, but in lieu of that just move to a place where you are around other grouchies and you'll be just fine. Of course, this geographic list applies only to poor lesbians, rich lesbians live in Miami and vacation in the following:

## Crunchy

1. Provincetown, MA
2. Park Slope (aka Dyke Slope), Brooklyn
3. Berkeley/Oakland
4. Seattle
5. Northhampton, MA
6. The entire state of New Mexico
7. Ithaca, NY

## Grouchy

1. East Village/Lower East Side
2. East Hollywood
3. Portland
4. Mission District/South of Market
5. Berlin or Prague

# Academy

Suppose you are a teen and you've realized that you are a dyke. Now you are faced with the dilemma, "Where do I go to college to be where the dykes are?" Weep no more, here are the top ten:

1. **Yale.** One word: *J-O-D-I-E.* Two more words: *S-A-R-A G-I-L-B-E-R-T.*

2. **Any of "The Seven Sisters" schools (Barnard, Smith, Mount Holyoke, Bryn Mawr, Wellesley, Vassar, and Radcliffe).** When they are not producing first ladies, this group of schools has also produced the most lesbian alums—Elizabeth Bishop, Ruth Benedict, and Carole Maso—to name a few and would be the first choice if it weren't for *J-O-D-I-E.*

3. **Oberlin.** Rumor has it that the school has perfected a special dyke cloning machine; for every one lesbian who enters, three more graduate, and they all look exactly the same.

4. **University of California (Santa Cruz).** It's where Judith Butler teaches and a nice cup of herbal tea is never more than a few Birkenstock-steps away.

5. **Sarah Lawrence.** Nobody can actually name a lesbian who is a Sarah Lawrence alum, it's just that legend has always had it that this is where lesbians go.

6. **Duke University.** The most liberal school in the South despite being in Jesse Helms's backyard. Has active gay and lesbian studies program.

7. **Stanford.** A women's sports powerhouse.

8. **SUNY Purchase.** A favorite among drama and film lesbians. *Beware!!!*

9. **Evergreen State College** (Olympia, WA). It's where Riot Grrrls come from.

10. **Lock Haven University** (Lock Haven, PA). It's where gym teachers come from.

There are two types of lesbians when it comes to sports—the girljock and the slackerdyke. Should a slacker find herself dating a jock she will constantly be begged, cajoled, and prodded into joining all the lesbian games. Here's a handy primer to the most common lesbian pasttimes for those who ditched PE to smoke in the girl's room.

## The top five sports, in order of popularity are:

1. Softball
2. Golf
3. Tennis
4. Swimming
5. Bowling and field hockey (tie)

## Crib notes for the Slackerdyke

### Softball

*As a spectator:* Sit in the stands with a cooler filled with beer or some other alcoholic substance, because watching softball is nearly as exciting as watching grass grow. *Do not* cheer for any of the players, rather boo and jeer the umps. This will save embarrassment when you become too intoxicated to sort things out and cheer when the opposing team scores the winning run. Also saves you from having to learn the rules of the game.

*As a player:* Softball was invented so that people could play baseball while drunk. You should be okay if you follow two simple rules, play the outfield (lots of standing around and little work) and, should you make contact with the ball while batting, always run in a counterclockwise direction.

### Golf

*As a spectator:*
A. Golf courses are the only place where driving under the influence is still permitted, therefore, the most fun to be

had in the sport of golf is to load up the cart with a ton of the micro bottles of beer sold at the clubhouse and drink them in one gulp while playing bumper cars with the party in front of you.

B.  Make crop circles in the fairway rough with ruts carved from your cart wheels.
C.  Put the cart pedal to the metal and whiz down the golf course at top speed yelling "fore" at every party until you clear the course.
D.  Continually ask all the caddies in your party if they ever saw *Caddyshack*.

*As a player:* We do not recommend that you ever play golf. Just because your girlfriend is dumb enough to waste her time playing such a stupid game, doesn't mean you should sink that low!

## Tennis

*As a spectator:* Tennis is not a fun spectator sport. The umpire is always yelling at you to shut up just when the match gets interesting and your neck gets sore from following the ball.
*As a player:* Should you find yourself forced into a game of doubles with your partner, win points by distracting your opponents during service by yelling, "Isn't that Martina over there?"

## Swimming

*As a spectator:* Rest easy if your girlfriend is into this because swimming is not a spectator sport.
*As a player:* Pretend that you are going to swim and then excuse yourself to sit in the sauna. Scope out the sauna for a new girlfriend or trick. Chances are that if she stays in the sauna for a good while, she's a slacker too.

## Bowling

Bowling is neither a spectator nor a participation sport, in fact it is not even a sport it's just an excuse to get drunk and wear stupid shoes that don't belong to you. If you're a true slackerdyke, this is behavior which requires no practice as it comes naturally.

## Field Hockey

Field hockey is just a good reason for participants to run around in short skirts and wield a club. Players are unusually ferocious and the ball is very hard so it hurts a lot if it hits you. Participate at your own risk. For the slacker, field hockey should remain only a spectator sport. However, as a spectator sport, it is highly recommended. It's like WASP female mud wrestling.

Being a dyke in a pop-culture-obsessed world means that you find your-self strangely drawn to those artifacts tossed aside, spit on, or that somehow seem like they don't fit into the otherwise breezy, carefree, celebrity world. We outcasts gotta look out for one another and when no one else seems to care, lesbians will always carry a torch for the most bizarre collection of media figures. How many times have we se-cretly scanned tabloids looking for the latest dirt or reluctantly admitted our fascination with any one of the following unlikely public figures:

## Tonya Harding

There is absolutely nothing redeemable about her, but who cares? We like her cause she's just so completely bad. Didn't your heart just bleed when she was caught on videotape complaining to the tow truck driver who was about to haul her pickup truck away?

## Amy Fisher

The victim of a teenage crush gone awry. She's mean, she's manipula-tive, she's possibly even crazy, but didn't we all jump for joy when her supposed lesbian lover from jail appeared on "Hard Copy"?

## Sara Gilbert

As the grumpy, wisecracking daughter on "Roseanne," she is the biggest dyke teen idol ever (well, it's not like there's a lot of competition in this category). We even sat through that horrible movie, *Poison Ivy,* just to watch her with sister cult idol, Drew Barrymore.

## Bessie Smith, Billie Holiday, Janis Joplin, and Patsy Cline

Different women, different time periods, but the appeal is basically the same. We revel in their troubles that somehow make our own seem less grave. It's this appeal that has made them cult figures for heartbroken, dejected depressives around the world. But the pain that flows through each of their voices, rings especially true to women fresh from their latest crushing defeat in the boxing ring of love.

## Amy Carter

No one else cares, but lesbians remain devoted to her principled, Ivy League, dropout jailbird ass. (By extension, lesbians also love Chelsea Clinton.)

## Anne Murray

Even mentioned on an episode of the TV sitcom "Empty Nest" where Carol (Dinah Manoff) remembers being seduced by a lesbian who invited her over to listen to Anne Murray records.

## Coco Chanel

Lesbians love Coco not just because she made chic little outfits and had a woman companion. She is revered by lipstick lesbians for her "Star Red," which is the only color lipstick should come in. (However, her past as a Nazi collaborator makes it difficult to elevate her.)

## Roger Corman and Russ Meyer

Roger Corman first won a place in the trash-loving lesbians' hall of fame for his film *Bloody Mama* (about a family of gangsters headed by the wild dykon Shelley Winters). He also directed *The Wild Angels,* a campy B movie about the fave dyke theme—female motorcycle gangs. Russ Meyer's fondness for supervixens, strippers, and cat fights has also earned him a place in the hall of fame. Tura Satana, Star of *Faster, Pussycat Kill! Kill!,* is the coolest woman ever to be captured on celluloid. Although he directed many films, consensus has it that *Faster Pussycat Kill! Kill!* is the one to see if you can only sit through one.

## Edie

Edie Sedgwick was *the* face of the Youthquake that shook the world in the sixties. She's the Andy Warhol look-alike who will remain forever famous for, among other things, being found in a bathroom in a compromising position with another girl at a party that attendee Mrs. Pat Buckley described as "disgusting."

## Jeff Stryker

Yes, he's a man and yes, he looks like he's made of plastic. But that's his appeal. He didn't need to market his own dildo, he is like a living breathing dildo in Teflon perfection.

## Peggy Lee

Gay men have Judy, but lesbians take Peggy Lee as their dissipated lounge chanteuse of choice.

## Karen Carpenter

Oddly she was rarely pictured with a male beau and almost always with other women, but let's not get carried away here. She was a bitchin' drummer, and her voice was so sad it just made you want to cry a river.

## Supermodel Gia

She was bold, beautiful, and beneath it all butch, but didn't she look stunning in a dress?

## Jan Brady/Tracy Partridge

Role models for a brain-dead generation—Jan has grunge appeal and Tracy has party-girl appeal. They were both the coolest women on seventies TV.

## Vampires

Why is it that lesbians love to watch movies that portray them as vampires? Why is it that mainstream films like to portray lesbians as vampires? Could it be that the original female vampire was Countess Elisabeth Bathory who was known to prey on young maidens? Perhaps, but vampire flicks are among the most enjoyable pop garbage. Check out Andrea Weiss's book *Vampires and Violets: Lesbians in Film* for more than you would ever need to know about the phenomenon of lesbian vampires in the cinema.

**Frida Kahlo**

Depressing and, by most standards, ugly art, yet she's a hero. Maybe it's those eyebrows.

**Stevie Nicks**

Though she denies rumors that she is a bisexual wicca member, she was a coke addicted rock'n'roll woman who wrote a bizarre love song about her bandmate's girlfriend Sara and a haunting song about a Welsh witch named Rhiannon. She makes Kate Bush look like Samantha Stevens.

**Heidi Fleiss**

She's a jailed pill queen who made her living as a madam, but all those rumors about a videotape of her, a girlfriend, and a dildo made her a heroine.

**Drew Barrymore**

Drew has told many interviewers how much she loves her girlfriends, but the apotheosis of the little girl lost came when she kissed Sara Gilbert in *Poison Ivy* and then told the media how much she loved

## FIVE "SURE-FIRE" WAYS TO TELL IF YOUR FAVORITE SINGER/ACTRESS/COMEDIENNE IS "ON THE TEAM":

1. She always tells interviewers that her private life is "private."
2. She never uses the pronoun "he" in songs (unless it's an old standard).
3. She talks a lot about her cats.
4. She gets married, but buys her female "personal assistant" a wedding present.
5. Reviewers constantly remark on her lack of "chemistry" with male co-stars.

doing it. For making us suffer through an otherwise awful movie, she redeemed herself by playing the downtrodden girl who gets revenge in Tamara Davis's version of *Guncrazy*. Lesbians don't just love Drew, they worship her.

### Janet Reno

Part John Wayne, part Perry Mason with a pinch of Wilt the Stilt, and presto you've got one big bad butch mama of an attorney general. Yeah, she had her minions burn down Koresh's digs, but this reincarnation of the axe-wielding teetotaler Carry Nation has become a friend to struggling women everywhere through her vigorous prosecution of deadbeat fathers who owe child support.

### Dee Dee Meyers

How do you know there's a whole new generation running the country? The press secretary was named Dee Dee. Really, she was supposed to be very smart and have an in-depth knowledge of politics, but who can believe that when she began a press briefing by telling reporters about how her relatives in California fared in the most recent earthquake or when during an appearance on "The Tonight Show" she gave John Travolta a Vinnie Barbarino doll?

### Mary Matalin

No, not the to-die-for, hearing-impaired actress, that's Marlee Matlin. I mean Rush Limbaugh's minion, conservative CNBC talk-show host and best-selling author, Mary Matalin. On "The Tonight Show" she demonstrated that she had a killer left hook when she punched out a Democratic donkey figure as part of a Leno skit. However, on her show, "Equal Time," she makes lethargic look like a hyperactive kid on a sugar high as she slouches back in her chair and drawls out sarcastic comment after witty aside in her slow, gravelly voice that only a true Brenda Vaccaro lover can appreciate. She's so cool that she can even turn a die-hard liberal into a fan.

### Kennedy

MTV's "Alternative Nation" veejay looks like a librarian's wet dream in her dorky glasses and if you think that is an insult, you're dead wrong 'cause that's her appeal. Usurping Martha Quinn's throne, Kennedy is now the nerdy quirky veejay heartthrob of dykes across the world.

## Women-in-Prison

Following an age-old formula that almost every lesbian finds grudgingly seductive—the new innocent little nymphet thrown into a pit of hard-boiled lifers eager to take advantage of her naiveté. Women-in-prison flicks are a secret vice. First popular among the drive-in set of the fifties, the genre was resurrected again in the exploitation crazed seventies. For smart, witty revisions of the genre check out Jonathan Demme's *Caged Heat* or *Reform School Girls* directed by Tom De Simone and starring Wendy O. Williams.

## Helen Hunt

She's first choice to play Dee Dee Meyers in the film version of the Clinton years. Every woman, straight or gay, probably has a crush on the "Mad About You" star and Nike spokesmodel. Before landing her role as the smart, semislacker, wisecracking wife of a documentary filmmaker, Hunt played everything from a girl flipped out on angel dust on an ABC "Afterschool Special" to a teenage good witch in another made-for-TV movie. Which of course, only makes us love her more.

## Supermodels

While it has been against every grain of pc dogma passed down to the current generation of lesbians, we are virtually obsessed with supermodels. Our mental clippings file is piled with numerous ads where Linda, Naomi, Cindy, Kristen McMenamy, and Christy Turlington cross-dress, pose with other women in "lesbian" scenes, or do things that somehow feed our mostly unfounded belief that all supermodels are lesbians. We have all watched George Michael's "Freedom '90" video obsessively for years and endlessly debated the relative merits of each model. But, empty speculation aside, models are indeed part of the contemporary lesbian experience.

First there was Gia Carangi, then there was Cindy Crawford's photo spread with k.d. lang in *Vanity Fair,* and now we have model and professional gal pal Ingrid Casares and butch poster girl Jenny Shimizu to claim as our own. As the number of photos taken of Jenny's wrench tattoo rises into the stratosphere, we watch with pride as she cavorts in print with boys, girls, and Kate Moss, silently hoping all the while for the fall of capitalism, the end of sexist oppression, or whatever it was that we thought would happen when one of our own became a model.

## Queen Latifah

Her female-positive raps first made her a hero, then she starred in a sitcom that resurrected the career of Tootie (Kim Fields) and she was enshrined but what put her into the realm of the truly divine was when she stated her interest in bankrolling a women's basketball league.

## Janeane Garofalo

As a grouchy pc comedienne who has the nerve to criticize *Show Girls* honcho Joe Eszterhas on network television she is without a doubt the coolest chick alive and that's why we love her.

## Courtney Love

Never has one woman elicited such scorn, contempt, admiration, and devotion from her audience. Whatever anyone thinks about her personal problems, one has to admit that watching her push her dyke drummer Patty Schemel to the floor and, in front of a stunned SNL audience, proceed to make out with her on national television makes her the queen of the universe, not only because she promotes lesbian visibility, but she gets to kiss dyke heartthrob Patty Schemel in the process.

READING IS FUNDAMENTAL . . .

## What Is Lesbian Literature?

You might think this is an easy question. However, there's still enough controversy surrounding it to keep the queer intelligentsia fighting about it. Dorothy Allison, an out proud lesbian who has written extensively in dyke fiction and non-fiction forums, became a flashpoint for this argument when her novel, *Bastard Out of Carolina,* was published to great critical acclaim. Because the content was not overtly lesbian, the book went unnominated by the Lambda Literary Awards, the "Academy Award" of queer literature.

As straight media has begun to pay more attention to lesbian and gay issues, the literature of our people has gained greater exposure as well. People like Sarah Schulman (see below) have been in the forefront of advocating for queer writing to "get out of the ghetto," doing readings in "mainstream" bookstores, agitating for more reviews, and generally getting in the publishing industry's face. Others in the industry have said on record that there is no "crossover" audience: that straight people simply don't buy gay books.

With this said, let's examine the question of what makes a work "lesbian."

## 1. Lesbian literature is anything written by a lesbian.

This is fine, except we don't always know who the lesbians are. If X is a lesbian, and writing work which isn't queer in content, how will anyone ever know? Of course, what will probably happen is after her death, X will be gently brought out of the closet and held up to great esteem. Dissertations will be written. Canons will be formed. So we'll know, eventually. Also, if you're on your toes, you'll notice that many lesbian and gay bookstores carry work by women who have never come out. If you read the book, and there's even an inkling of dyke about it, it's a safe bet the author is a sister of Sappho. People who run bookstores know these things.

The other problem with this definition (for some) is the fact that some lesbians don't write about lesbians. Mary Renault was a lesbian, living with a woman lover for sixty-some-odd years, yet wrote only one book about women. The rest of her work consisted primarily of historical novels set in the ancient world, always of love between men. So is this "lesbian literature?" What about women who write about straight love? How much of this work is informed by a lesbian sensibility?

Let's look at another formulation.

## 2. Lesbian literature is anything that has a lesbian in it.

This is a sticking point for a lot of people. Some might say it's like saying *Basic Instinct* is a lesbian/bisexual movie. And a few recent books might bear that out: books that have lesbians or lesbian affairs in them, yet have no relation to that vague, "I know it when I see it" dyke aesthetic (see below). *Even Cowgirls Get the Blues* is a good case in point. Tom Robbins is not a lesbian. He is a man. He even might be straight. But *Cowgirls* has gained another audience among queer women for Robbins's novel of (among other things) cowdyke love. But then again, it's not a love story per se. So what's a girl to do?

(We're getting closer. Relax.)

## 3. Lesbian literature is anything that is written by a lesbian, and/or has lesbians in it, and passes your individual test of "lesi-ness."

By Georgia, I think we've got it.

# The "So You Want to Be a Lesbian?" Eclectic, Biased, and Annotated Guide to Lesbian Literature as Defined Above

### Historically important, "hoity-toity" writers that you're going to need to read if you want to break into the intellectual mafia:

**Djuna Barnes:** Djuna was quite the looker in her day. She moved in the trés chic circles of Parisian lesbians that held court during the 1920s and 1930s, mostly run by American women (with the aforementioned buttload of money). Djuna established her eternal place on bookshelves with *Nightwood*. While not nearly as self-loathing as *The Well of Loneliness* (see below), it can be awfully dense, due to the influence of the Surrealists. Barnes's other big Sapphic tome is *Ladies Almanack,* which is a series of thinly veiled portraits of the Parisian Lesbians she hung around with, some more savage than others. Unfortunately, without a good history book, it doesn't make much sense to the average nineties girl.

**Jane Bowles:** An excellent writer on her own, she has often been overshadowed by her husband Paul. Husband, you say? Well, they were both queer (See Vita Sackville-West) and often even strange. Her work has been both villifed and praised, but one must read it for oneself. Unfortunately, her life was even sadder and stranger than her fiction.

**Rita Mae Brown:** Rita Mae truly set the world on its ear when *Rubyfruit Jungle* was published. One of the first works to present a lesbian who wasn't institutionalized, or close to being there, where her problems were mostly how people reacted to her, not how she dealt with her sexuality, it broke through the disease model of lesbian literature. Read now in the light of "the gay nineties," it still holds up because it's a good read: great characters, good love stories, and the always reliable me-against-the-world theme that makes you root for Molly Bolt up to the last page. You should read this book. Period.

As for Ms. Brown's other work, well, it's been interesting. *Sudden Death* is supposedly a fictionalization of her relationship with Martina Navratilova. Her latest books are wildly divergent. *Venus Envy* is seen as the closest thing to a followup *Rubyfruit* has. If it is, it's pretty disappointing. The characters are almost universally unlikable stereotypes, gay and straight alike, the plot is thin, and Brown's insistence on alerting us to her more-than-passing acquaintance to Latin and Greek language and mythology becomes ridiculous as she brings in the Greek gods and goddesses to have sex with and teach the protagonist that life is joyous. *Dolly* is a historical novel based on the life of Dolley Madison. You make the call.

**Willa Cather:** Willa dressed in men's clothing, called herself "William" for a time, and fell desperately in love with a woman. However, there is nothing overtly lesbian about her work. Nonetheless, her books are good reading and staples of the American canon.

**Simone DeBeauvoir:** Through contemporary biography, we have come to learn that Simone was about as oppressed as any woman, despite her own best knowledge. We also begin to have some insight into her relationships with other women, which may or may not have been more than sororal. For the mere act of writing *The Second Sex,* she deserves homage. For putting up with that lout Jean-Paul, she deserves a medal.

**H.D. (Hilda Doolittle):** A poet and writer, H.D. was an American expatriate, whose lesbian novels have only recently been published. As a bisexual woman, she carried on in ways that those of us who will never get the chance to expatriate can only envy. *Paint It To-Day* and her poems are her most overt works.

**Radclyffe Hall:** This is a given. Everyone's read *The Well of Loneliness,* or says they have. It's one of the most written about books in the genre, and unfortunately, it's incredibly dated. Not to jump on the bandwagon of espousing only "positive images for homosexual people," but this book would lead you to believe we're all really depressed, unhappy with our gender, and have a buttload of money so we can live in suits and ties and hunt all the time.

**Radclyffe Hall** (posing with her dog Colette), *the* Butch of English letters. One of the major saints in the lesbian canon, she should be invoked against sloppy dressing, run-on sentences, and cats who shed too much.

**Audre Lorde:** One of the mothers of lesbian feminism, her work is a testament to the power and strength of the women's movement, and the movement of women of color. One of her best works is *Zami: A New Spelling of My Name* which deals with her growing up and coming out in New York City. Her poetry and essays (especially *Sister Outsider*) are required reading.

**Carson McCullers:** A very intense writer, whose tales of tomboys and truly bizarre Southerners (at least to Northerners) are fascinatingly written. *The Heart Is a Lonely Hunter* is probably her most famous work.

**Isabel Miller:** *Patience and Sarah,* a staple of lesbian fiction, is the story of two women in love in a Puritan farm community. Rumor had it that if Jodie Foster and Kelly McGillis hadn't worked out on *The Accused,* this was the film they were going to make instead.

**Gloria Naylor:** Just because you watched *The Women of Brewster Place* on television with Miss Oprah, that doesn't mean you're off the hook. A good novel, with one of the more sad yet ultimately triumphant endings among these books.

**Jane Rule:** A good test for a first date is to ask them which woman they thought was hotter in *Desert Hearts,* based on Rule's *Desert of the Heart*—Helen Shaver or Patrice Charbonneau. (The latter insisted on taking her darn baby to every public appearance supporting the movie. She should have just worn a shirt that said "SEE, I FUCK MEN!") You should read the book, too. Ms. Rule has also published essay collections and other works of fiction with Naiad (see below).

**Vita Sackville-West:** Let's be honest for a moment shall we? Vita's sex life is infinitely more interesting than her fiction. But if you're making your way in the lesbian studies crowd, you may want to dive into it.

**May Sarton:** One of the Grande Dames of Lez Lit, her relentless journal keeping kept Norton in material for over three decades. Best known for her autobiographical writing, she also wrote novels. Sarton died in 1995.

**Getrude Stein:** An icon for us all. Our patron saint. People name cats after her, which is a lofty tribute from the kind of people who call their pets "animal life companions." Unfortunately, a lot of readers might find it difficult to understand what it is exactly she represents. The content of her work is not particularly sapphic, and some people who are appreciative of things like, oh, punctuation and narrative have a hard time discerning exactly what she's talking about. An example from "Tender Buttons":

*DINING*
*Dining is west.*

Meaning is up for grabs here. Note, however, that *The Autobiography of Alice B. Toklas* (Gertie's gal-pal), probably her most widely read work, is pretty accessible, and sometimes downright chatty.

**Monique Wittig:** This is what happens when French feminism, philosophy, linguistics, and lesbianism intersect. Wittig's best-known books, *Les Guérrillères* and *The Lesbian Body*, envision a language, a body, and (in the former book) a world where women are not bound by the old order, but overthrow it (by force). *Les Guérrillères* invokes the names of women throughout the narrative of the destruction of the old world, for example:

> *FLORA ZITA SAVA CORNELIA*
> *DRAUPADI JULIENNE ETMEL*
> *CHLOE DESDEMONA RAPHAELLA etc.*

**Gertrude Stein** (l) and **Alice B. Toklas** (r) inspired many writers and artists both through Gertrude's patronage and Alice's cooking. Perhaps the most famous lesbian couple of all time, they have been honored by millions (and we mean MILLIONS) of lesbians who, in their honor, have named their cats after them.

Wittig has made an important contribution to feminist philosophy here by letting us know that in the revolution, there will be no Muffys.

**Virginia Woolf:** Those people less inclined to reading (about 90 percent of the population at last count) might know "Ginny" best from the Sally Potter film, *Orlando*. Didja see it? Yeah, well originally it was a book. Quite a good one. Actually, it was written as a love treasure to Ms. Vita Sackville-West. She and Mrs. Woolf were "as one" for a time. Virginia also wrote important books like *Mrs. Dalloway* and *A Room of One's Own*. She was also immortalized by Edward Albee as the title character in the play *Who's Afraid of Virginia Woolf?*, the movie version of which starred Elizabeth Taylor. She did not play Virginia Woolf. No one played Virginia Woolf, since she does not appear in the play, causing great consternation to people in Modern American Drama classes, who fake their way through essays on it, only to receive failing grades.

## The Naiad Years

Many readers may remember the first "gay" book they read: *Rubyfruit Jungle, Desert of the Heart,* or perhaps *Summer in Sodom*. What many lesbians may have in common is that their first lesbian book was published by Naiad Press. Being one of the few publishers committed to

BETTMANN ARCHIVES

**Vita Sackville-West** (l) was famous for her writing and her gardens. Her affair with Violet Trefusis was steamy, stormy, and out of control. (Their love letters make great crib notes for the romantically impaired.)

putting lesbian work out for readers for quite some time (along with Rising Tide, Firebrand, Cleis, Banned Books, New Victoria, and Diana), they were there when everyone else was sitting on their butts, waiting around for the queer sky to fall on them.

Now, of course, with so many publishers having hopped onto the still sparsely populated bandwagon, Naiad has seen some rough talk about their books: "The cover art is dreadful," "The books are schlocky," and "If I read one more coming out story I'm going back in."

But taking a contextual view of Naiad can help put all of this into perspective. They never claimed to be Random House. They were doing work on a shoestring budget when there were so few others even looking at lesbian fiction. Sure, they're low budget, but there's a certain pleasure to be had from a sort of grade-B dyke book. They published Sarah Schulman's first novel, and last but not least, they have reprinted the *Beebo Brinker* saga, the kin of *Tales of the City* for the fifties and early sixties Greenwich Village lesbian set. So understanding where Naiad stands in this history, here is the Hall of Fame for the Naiad Years:

**Ann Bannon:** *Beebo Brinker* series (comparable to *Melrose Place*)

**Sarah Dreher:** Western romances

**Katherine V. Forrest:** Mysteries, one of which is supposedly going to be a film entitled *The Nightwood Bar,* starring Mary Louise Parker. However, just remember that *The Front Runner* has been in "pre-production" for something like twenty years.

**Penny Hayes:** Westerns

**Karin Kallmaker:** Romances

**Evelyn Kennedy:** Romances

**Lee Lynch:** Midwestern butch/femme love stories

**Jane Rule:** (See above)

**Ann Allen Shockley:** An African-American writer whose books are romances with social pertinence

# Boomtown in Dykeville

It was only a matter of time, someone was bound to figure it out. "There's gold in them thar dykes." (Little do they know that we really don't have much money and we're up to our necks in veterinary bills, but nevermind.) So the eighties and nineties have seen a boomlet in mainstream publishing about gay and lesbian issues, mostly the former, but the latter as well. You would think that said boomlet would lead to more quality fiction getting into more bookstores, with more women making money and more readers finishing books with satisfied looks on their faces.

Well, yes and no.

## The Good:

**Sarah Schulman:** The *mater* of it all. With six novels and a collection of her journalism writings, she has seemingly broken through the sisterly ghetto to get widespread recognition for her books of New York dykes. In order they are:

> ***The Sophie Horowitz Story:*** A cartoonish version of the Kathy Boudin–Brinks Robbery
> ***Girls, Visions and Everything:*** An *hommage* to Jack Kerouac involving a women's theater group that seems pretty similar to NYC's WOW, but is one of the best renderings of East Village lesbian life.
> ***After Delores:*** Schulman's own favorite work, a murder mystery tied up with the anguish of a breakup.
> ***People in Trouble:*** A work centering on how activism (à la ACT UP) transforms the lives of those involved in it.
> ***Empathy:*** A story of love and Freudianism.
> ***Rat Bohemia:*** Love with a dyke exterminator on the Lower East Side.

These books are must-reads.

**Dorothy Allison:** As discussed above, *Bastard Out of Carolina* became a litmus test for those arguing over what makes lesbian fiction. It is a great novel, no matter where you fall on the question. In addition, we are all lucky to have her essays collected in *Skin: Talking About Sex, Class, and Literature,* as well as *Trash* (her short stories) and *The Women Who Hate Me* (poetry). Dorothy is a national treasure.

---

**Kathy Acker:** Is it lesbian? Is it fiction? What the heck is she doing? (Right now, she's doing bodybuilding and getting tattooed a lot.) A voice for women who are pissed off, angry, filled with punk attitude and ready to tear down literature as we know it, Acker's work is a favorite among Generation X slacker girls with nowhere to go but down.

**Carol Anshaw:** If you're one of those queer women who hates swimming and the whole culture surrounding it, don't dismiss *Aquamarine* right off the bat. It's more than a book about cruising poolside. It's a wonderful look at the "what ifs" in life, and written with great feeling.

**Rebecca Brown:** With two books of short stories from City Lights under her belt, Ms. Brown has launched herself into the arena, and has taken a few blows. *Annie Oakley's Girl* contains a mix of moving, straightforward narratives that are poignant and stirring, along with some less traditional forms that might put off some readers. *Terrible Girls* earned some enmity among readers surveyed[1] primarily for the title story that can be summed up by: Woman cuts off her right arm, other woman blinds herself. They're stuck together. While this may be an apt metaphor for the "one-date, I'll-never-leave-you" relationship, on the page, it could actually make you laugh.

**Jane DeLynn:** Probably her best known dyke book is *Don Juan in the Village*, a collection of sexual encounters that some championed as an exploration of "our alienation from society and each other" (Kathy Acker) and "some of the most nakedly honest writing about lust I know of in contemporary fiction" (Brett Easton Ellis). If you're looking for shiny happy dykes in love, look elsewhere.

**Emma Donoghue:** This Irish *wunderkind* has written *Stir Fry*, a fun, lovely book about going off to college, sharing an apartment with a lesbian couple[2], and making "the" discovery about yourself. Expect to hear more from her.

**Leslie Feinberg:** A novel about growing up butch and working class, *Stone Butch Blues* pays tribute to those who came before Stonewall and women's liberation, and derived little benefit from ideology in a time when getting a job was most pressing. The protagonist goes through a portion of gender-reassignment surgery, then finds this wasn't the answer to the problem of a society that can't deal with difference. Feinberg is a labor and transgender activist, and the book is

---

[1] It was a very short survey, however. "What did you think of *Terrible Girls?*"
[2] Something the reader should beware. This always ends badly for at least one person. Caveat renter.

suffused with her personal and political experience; an important contribution to the silence on class and gender issues in the "community."

**Fannie Flagg:** You loved her on "Match Game 70"-something, and you loved the movie, even though it irked you that all those straight people were enjoying what you knew in your heart was a Southern butch-femme love story. Well, read *Fried Green Tomatoes at the Whistle Stop Cafe* and feel at least somewhat vindicated. Flagg produced a comic novel that will make you laugh, make you cry and perhaps even get you to make fried green tomatoes (recipe included.) This is the kind of book you can love, and so can your mother.

**A. M. Homes:** A writer of great talent, and flashes of real insight, as well as superior craftspersonship, she is perhaps unfortunately best known as the woman who wrote the Barbie story that started the literary anthology, *Mondo Barbie.* Aside from this great short story, she has two novels under her belt: *Jack,* the story of a young man dealing with his father's coming out, and *In a Country of Mothers,* a book of obsession and therapy.

**Jennifer Levin:** Her two books, *The Sea of Light* and *Water Dancer* use competitive swimming as the backdrop for stories of love and survival. Well-written and enthralling (especially *Water Dancer*).

**Heather Lewis:** *House Rules* changed what lesbian literature encompasses. While certainly evocative of "Brat Pack" writers when you read the jacket blurb (drugs, violence, sex, vacuous existence) get beyond the copywriting and go to the very dark heart of what Lewis gives you. The prose is frightening in its edgy sparseness; she says a great deal with seeming effortlessness.

**Mabel Maney:** This woman is a genius. Who else would take Nancy Drew, match her up with Cherry Ames (War Nurse), turn them loose with a butch/femme couple, and have them solve mysteries? The three books are a hoot and a half. The most recent, *The Ghost in the Closet,* features The Hardly Boys. These books are must-owns.

**Really Trashy Books You Shouldn't Read Unless You're Some Sort of Literary Masochist:**

***Loonglow,*** by Helen Eisenbach: If you're lucky you won't be able to find this, even if you try. However, it pops up on remainder piles frequently, so be careful. This is the overwrought story of a woman who gets dumped in a bar by her woman lover, and of the guy who overhears them. The two of them are wholly forgettable, but Mia D'Allessandro, the heart-breaker is so unbelievably "beautiful," "clever," and "enchanting" that you remember her name only because she's so constantly described and referred to. The worst part is, of course, the way the two opposite-sex characters end up together on the last page. Enough to make one take up a rocket launcher.

**Suicide Blonde,** by Darcy Steinke: A recent "let's jump on the lesbian chic bandwagon" book, the most redeeming part of this novel is it's setting (San Francisco). Somehow thought of by some as a lesbian novel, but there's more description of the woman's bisexual boyfriend's exploits than any sapphic displays, and there's actually someone named Madison. No dice.

**Playing with Fire,** by Dani Shapiro: Nice girl comes to college, falls in love with college roommate. They get it on, she goes home with her over vacation and finds out her girlfriend's having an affair with her father and loses it. Yikes. Turgid prose, implausible characters, and just generally painful reading.

**Great Writers Who Don't Really Fit Anywhere in Here but Should Be Mentioned:**

**Jacqueline Susann:** *Valley of the Dolls,* a masterpiece of blockbuster fiction, was more than just camp. It was also an exploration of lesbian desire (that part didn't make it into the movie). Jackie's life was a strange one, and her fiction certainly reflected it. Rumor had it that her suicide attempt was prompted by Ethel Merman's rejection of her affections. In *Once Is Not Enough,* the thinly veiled Garbo character has an affair with another woman. While Jackie certainly wasn't a poster child for lesbian fiction, she was at least getting it out there and into the faces of millions of readers.

**Fran Lebowitz:** A genius in her own right, we hope the release of the *Fran Lebowitz Reader* will help younger people know what it was that makes her a great American camp wit. While her seventies pieces have obviously aged, her dogged work (thirteen years and counting) on her novel, *Exterior Signs of Wealth,* promises to pay off when she finishes. In the meantime, try and catch one of her readings of her work in progress (think of it as *Finnegans Wake* for the nineties hipsters) and learn about humor. And smoking.

# FIVE BOOKS THAT WILL MAKE YOU HAPPY TO BE A LESBIAN:

***The Stepford Wives,*** by Ira Levin: Terrifying portrait of robotic housewives in the suburbs. If you watch late-night TV, catch the movie sequel, *The Stepford Children.*

***Madame Bovary,*** by Gustave Flaubert: Great literature, but all that agonizing over men? Please.

***How to Pick Up Girls:*** This book has been around since the seventies, and is advertised to this day in the back of men's magazines. An eerily accurate portrait of what guys think they need to do to get laid.

Any book by **Andrea Dworkin:** Sure, she's an advocate of censorship and has bad politics. But once you're done reading *Intercourse,* you'll never think about doing THAT again.

***The Joy of Lesbian Sex:*** Who knew there was all that you still hadn't done? Get to work, girlfriends.

"The history and politics of women-loving women is one which is written every day, yet can never be complete."

This profoundly cheezy statement holds an element of truth, whether you're a social constructionist or an essentialist.[1] With such a wide and diverse population, it's a good bet that someone's going to miss something somewhere. ("Oh, damn, no one ever documented that band of lesbians who worshipped Dick Clark back in the fifties.") With this said, let it be added that your humble authors are not historians nor do we play them on TV. So what follows is a view of American history that is at best eclectic and at worst, twisted. (See Lesbian Studies for a reading list, p. 195)

BETTMANN ARCHIVES

**The Salem witch trials:** One of the most disturbing phenomena to seventeenth-century New Englanders who saw a witch in every fireplace were women who were not "normal." No doubt some of those who were burned, tortured, drowned (and per-

**Janet Flanner,** a pivotal member of the Paris group of American expatriates and a great writer herself, onboard ship just before she set sail for Paris in 1923. Of course, what lay ahead was fame, good company, and . . . well . . . girls, girls, girls.

[1]Essentialists maintain that "lesbians" have existed throughout time as such. Social Constructionists assert that "lesbian" as an identity was created in the latter part of the nineteenth century and before that, while there were certainly lesbian acts, there was no real community to participate in.

haps even teased) by the courts at Salem had some sapphic leanings, which brought suspicion on them.

**"Romantic friendships"** or **"Boston marriages":** These phrases describe Victorian-era bonding between women, which could last a lifetime. Now known as "Northampton friendships," the seat of lesbianism having moved west across Massachusetts, the snogging is now above-board.

**"Passing" women:** Found throughout the history of the U.S.; there seemed to be a glut of them on the Western Frontier. These women who lived as men had wives, sometimes children, and supported their families by working in traditionally male jobs. Sometimes upon their death, they were revealed to be women, much to the horror of their spouses. (One might suspect that some of those spouses knew a little more than they were admitting to.)

**Glamour lesbians:** The original chic lesbians, they primarily lived in Paris during the 1920s and thirties. Most of them were well-off and spent their days going to salons, writing poetry, and sleeping with each other. (Ah, the good old days. . . . )

Germany, 1927—Sometimes a cigar is just . . . a cigar.

**Butch/Femme Couples:** The 1940s seemed to spawn these erotic identities, perhaps because of wartime employment of women in "masculine" jobs (even the armed forces), pants-wearing becoming slightly more acceptable, and the aftereffects of Garbo, Dietrich, and Hepburn. These identities flourished during the fifties and early sixties.

**The Homophile movement:** Begun in the 1950s, the movement's first organization was the Mattachine Society, which in turn spun off the Daughters of Bilitis. Oddly enough, even here the women began to want to hide the butches in the closet.

**The Women's liberation movement:** Gave us bra-burning, the antimakeup movement, street theater at the Miss America Pageant, and a wholly raised consciousness. Now, of course, we all know they also did their best to purge the dykes when scared men started screaming lesbian at them. (A lot of good that did.)

**The Gay liberation movement:** Spawned by the bar raid heard round the world, gay men began their own fight for equality. Lesbians often were at odds with their brothers, who had seemingly different priorities as well as some real problems relating to women. However, Anita Bryant's Save Our Children campaign, as well as the California Briggs Initiative, both seeking to bar gay teachers from the classroom, helped to build more bridges between them, as well as earn Anita Bryant a pie in the face from a gay man on national television. With the murder of Harvey Milk in San Francisco, just how enraged gay men and lesbians were became apparent to those who didn't or couldn't care less.

**The "Sex Wars":** The first shot was fired in 1982 (at the Barnard Conference on Sexuality, where women picketed other women presenting papers on such topics as S/M, pornography, and butch/femme), and the Sex Wars continued for almost a decade. No one has ever claimed victory or conceded defeat, but a good look at the ever-expanding lesbian porn section in the local queer bookstore might make you think the answer is obvious.

**AIDS:** The horrifying pandemic continues, seemingly unabated, but it mobilized lesbians to help gay men start community health projects, social service agencies, and direct-action organizations. While gay men suddenly woke up and realized that the rest of America didn't care whether they lived or died, a new political impetus fired up the communities to fight back.

**ACT UP/Queer Nation/Lesbian Avengers:** The late 1980s saw a community making more inroads toward banding together, as activism became more and more necessary to confront an apathetic government. Into the 1990s, the threat of local and statewide antigay referendums becomes greater and more grassroots groups are forming to fight these when needed.

## Recent Ugly Moments in Lesbian History and Politics

▼ During the campaign for Iowa's Equal Rights Amendment, Pat Robertson accuses supporters of encouraging women to "leave their husbands, kill their children, become lesbians, and practice witchcraft."

▼ The Dworkin-MacKinnon Act takes effect in Canada, thereby enabling customs to stop such dangerous and pornographic works as *The Lesbian and Gay Studies Reader, Hothead Paisan,* and the plays of Albert Innaurato.

▼ Roberta Achtenberg is nominated to the Department of Housing, only to set Jesse Helms off on another apoplectic fit of homophobia, vowing that no "admitted lez-bee-in" is going to be confirmed. (She was.)

▼ The Christian Right organizes statewide antigay initiatives, winning in Colorado. The law is struck down as unconstitutional and is being appealed to the Supreme Court.

▼ Whitney Houston marries Bobby Brown, giving her "personal assistant" Robyn Crawford a Mercedes as a consolation present.

▼ A woman living in Florida attends the March on Washington, only to find her house firebombed upon her return.

▼ Sharon Bottoms's mother brings suit against her daughter as an unfit parent, because she is a lesbian. Sharon wins the case, then loses it on appeal.

▼  Richard Gere places an ad in the London *Times,* proclaiming that he and his wife Cindy Crawford are both heterosexual. They separate a few months later.

▼  During the pre-Oscar publicity for her movie *Nell,* Jodie Foster takes to showing off her new live-in "boyfriend."

## Lesbian Politics

When you get a group of women together who believe devoutly in decentralizing leadership, consensus building, and consciousness raising, what have you got? Well, depending on who you're talking to either a recipe for disaster or the building blocks of the lesbian/gay/AIDS direct-action movements. Yes indeed, these cornerstones of feminist politics were in turn introduced in the eighties by those who knew it best, people (both women and men) who had worked in the civil rights, reproductive rights, and women's movements.

Proponents of lesbian politics have often had a difficult time articulating exactly what they meant. Whether it was the problem child of the women's movement or the ignored little sister of the gay men's movement, a lot of times working within the larger frameworks of these organizations was frustrating and enraging—at one point, lesbians held their own, separate pride marches in New York due to anger and problems with gay men.

During the 1970s, separatism was seen as an answer to these problems. Devoting all of one's energy and time to other lesbian women was not only a political statement, but you could stay out of all the capitalist patriarchy baloney. While there are still some practitioners and communes, for the most part separatism as a way of life has fallen by the wayside as politics of inclusion, direct action, or assimilation have begun to take up more and more time.

With the eighties came AIDS, which spawned AIDS activism, an in-your-face response to the sickness and death that came to many urban areas during that decade. Helping found ACT UP were older women with years of experience, as well as younger dykes who liked to scream and yell at inertia-prone politicians and homophobic religious leaders. Out of ACT UP came Queer Nation, which wanted to focus more on civil-rights issues and homophobia for lesbians and gay men (hence the word *Queer*). There was significant dissatisfaction among the women in Queer Nation when it came to having their views heard and represented. The Lesbian Avengers were born of these flames, and has seemingly taken over dyke politics in those areas of the country where it's active. Their actions have been as diverse as a Waltz-In on Valentine's Day, the successful Dyke Marches at the March on Washington and Stonewall 25, and the Lesbian Freedom Rides. A brief listing of national organizations, or those with chapters around the country, follows.

**National Gay and Lesbian Task Force:** It took them until the early eighties to add the words *and Lesbian* to their name. Now which word was so difficult . . . ? Organizes on a national level to fight for civil rights and against homophobia. Has been going through some rough periods since the departure of Urvashi Vaid: a number of lesbian executive directors (good) who didn't stick it out very long (bad or good, depending on which one you're talking about), massive departures, and now a controversial new executive who may or may not have been a guerrilla in Manila, making people a bit nervous about whither goes NGLTF.

**The Human Rights Campaign Fund** raises money to help candidates who are queer or queer friendly. A few of their choices have earned some well-deserved head scratching. The most annoying thing about them is their Congressional telegram campaign, where people harangue you to sign up at every Lesbian and Gay Pride event with more than twenty people, and you are approached by at least four of them in an hour.

**GLAAD: The Gay and Lesbian Alliance Against Defamation** has local chapters around the country, which monitor the media for negative images and fight for visibility of lesbians and gays. Some find them slightly reactionary, while others feel their "positive images" campaign left a lot to be desired.

**ACT UP:** A collection of local organizations. Some are more active than others; it depends on what is happening locally, as well as burnout and (sadly) deaths, which have both hurt membership. With the Republicans gearing up for some nastiness, expect a rejuvenated ACT UP to get in there and kick some butt.

**Queer Nation:** A collection of local chapters. Difficulties with interorganizational politics, as well as the politics of inclusion, have made some chapters almost wholly inactive. Sometimes snidely referred to as "Queer Inertia."

**Lesbian Avengers:** A collection of local chapters. This is where the action is right now—seemingly populated by young, energetic lesbians who want to change the world and aren't yet jaded or cynical enough to quit. Go for the cruising, stay for the fight.

**Dyke Action Machine:** Not so much a political group as art activism. By coopting popular images (GAP ads, Calvin Klein underwear ads, movie posters) and subverting them with lesbian content, they change the urban landscape for the better.

**America Online:** Not a political group, but a computer-information service with an active lesbian and gay population. Good resource for political and social information.

**Queer Resources Directory:** Another computer information stop in the Internet. Reachable by telnet: vector.casti.com (see Resource Guide: Web Sites, p. 222).

## The Future of Lesbian Politics

With the results of the 1994 elections things are looking pretty bleak for us. The defeat of Clinton's attempt to lift the military ban on gays seems to have been the last time he took any interest in lesbian and gay issues. Of course the Republicans are *very* interested, for all the wrong reasons.

Don't be surprised to see more statewide and local antigay initiatives. More wars about multicultural education that includes gay men and lesbians. More homophobia sanctioned by the courts. Less tolerance.

So what's a girl to do?

Well, you can stand and fight in whatever way you see fit. Contribute time, money, and skills. Chain yourself to Newt Gingrich. Off Jesse Helms. Run for local office. Kiss your girlfriend in the street. Come out to your boss. Write letters to the local newspapers. Throw pies at Rush Limbaugh.

Or if some awful Republican wins the presidential election in 1996, you may want to examine asylum opportunities in Scandinavia. Just kidding.

## Powerdyke:

Though there has been a crossover, this type is often butch. The powerdyke leans toward men's suits by expensive designers, fashionable accessories, and an occasional cigar smoked in bars with red velvet walls and a billiards room (as opposed to a pool table). Inexplicably, she is often seen keeping company with Jock Girls. Many Powerdykes work in the communications field, while others just dress up on weekends. The less expensive, more casual version would be the "Gap Dyke."

# SELECTED GUIDE TO DYKE, DYKE-THEMED, AND BELOVED-BY-DYKES FILM

## Art Films

There is a common perception that art films are boring, slow moving, ponderous, and difficult to watch. As a dyke-film buff, one will find it necessary to cast this belief aside (and reclaim the derogatory connotation that goes with the word *art*) since many of the best films made by lesbian directors or that have dyke themes are, perish the thought, independently produced ART films. So, for the times when you just want to feel good about yourself, watch a film made by a lesbian independent director. They don't ask you to read against the grain and feel bad that you like an ideologically circumspect film. The combination of arty technique and psychologically complex characters produce films or videos that are both politically correct (in the best sense) and art.

**Damned if You Don't** (1987). Directed by Su Friedrich. Black-and-white experimental film about a young woman who lives out many a lesbian's secret fantasy and seduces a nun.

**Daughters of the Dust** (1991). Directed by Julie Dash. Dash's magnificent chronicle of several generations of women in an African-American family follows the trials of Yellow Mary, family member who was identified in the reviews as lesbian.

**Even Cowgirls Get the Blues** (1994). Directed by Gus Van Sant. A bizarre art film adaptation of a quasi-lesbian novel by Tom Robbins. It stars Uma Thurman and Rain Phoenix with a host of Hollywood celebs dropping by the all-girl ranch for a little fun. (Added bonus: the score is by k.d. lang.)

**Go Fish** (1994). Directed by Rose Troche. A sexy and uncomfortably all too true to life film about lesbian life in the nineties.

***Jollies,*** et al. (1990). Directed by Sadie Benning. Made with a Fisher-Price Pixel video camera when she was in her late teens, all of Benning's tapes about being a dyke teen living in Any Town, USA trace the evolution of her sexuality from the twins she liked in kindergarten, to Barbie dolls and girlie bracelets, to the day she so longs for when people will look at her as she walks the streets and say "That's a dyke."

***Lesbian Humor*** and ***Lesbian Sexuality***. Two compilations of the films of Barbara Hammer available on videotape. *Lesbian Humor* contains six films including *Superdyke* about a bunch of Amazon super heroes, while *Lesbian Sexuality* has four including her much acclaimed *Dyketactics*.

***Mayhem*** (1987). Directed by Abigail Child. Part of her "Is this What You Were Born For?" series of films that explores cinematic genres and gender issues, *Mayhem* is a lush black-and-white experimental film about lesbians and gender stereotypes.

***No Skin Off My Ass*** (1991). Directed by Bruce LaBruce. Captures the trials and tribulations of queer punk "love" and features dyke punk legend G. B. Jones. (Also worth seeking out are Jones's own films like *Lollipop* and the *Yo Yo Gang*.)

***The Right Side of My Brain*** (1984). Directed by Richard Kern. For an artsy look at a rock star flirting with the lesbian continuum check out this Lydia Lunch tour de force. The film is about a young woman trying to make sense of her descent into a hellish sex underworld and ends with an almost tender S/M scene between Lunch and Sally Ven Yu Berg.

***She Must Be Seeing Things*** (1988). Directed by Sheila McLaughlin. This is a love story of two professional dykes, Jo and Agatha. One becomes obsessively jealous after reading the other's diaries and begins to stalk her lover in male drag. (McLaughlin also directed *Committed* [1984] with writer Lynne Tillman about the life of Frances Farmer.)

***The Virgin Machine*** (1988). Directed by Monika Treut. The saga of a woman in search of love whose travels take her from Germany to San Francisco where the film is hijacked by the wacky Susie Bright showing off her dildo collection. (Also worth seeing is Treut's *My Father Is Coming* [1991].)

# Films That Have a Cult Following or
# Are Merely Beloved by Lesbians

Cult films divide up into two groups, there are those that are not only good, but good for you, and that is why they become popular (like *Lianna* or *Personal Best*). There are also those that are so truly trashy that they're great! Bad films are the visual equivalent of junk food, and almost always make lesbian characters into sickos, wackos, perverts, and degenerates. But they sure are fun to watch!

***Beyond the Valley of the Dolls*** (1970). Directed by Russ Meyer. Written by Roger Ebert (of, yes, Siskel and Ebert). An all-girl band called the Carrie Nations hits Hollywood to make it in the big time. One of the bandmembers becomes a girltoy to an older dyke fashion designer. The two women are then murdered by a crazed, record producer transvestite, Z-man, who beheads his boyfriend for good measure. The carnage finally ends when Z-man is killed in a struggle with the remaining Carrie Nations.

***The Bitter Tears of Petra van Kant*** (1973). Directed by Rainer Werner Fassbinder. A slow-moving yet gripping drama about a cruel relationship between a fashion designer and her star model, who has difficulty leaving her male friends behind. Highlight: Petra crying to her lover, "Lie to me! Yes!"

***Black Widow*** (1987). Directed by Bob Rafelson. Theresa Russell and Debra Winger star in this crime thriller about an FBI agent (Winger) on the trail of a murderess (Russell) who marries men only to dispose of them serially shortly after the final vows in order to acquire their mountains of money. The two women become embroiled in a seduction plot and the sexual tension between Russell and Winger threatens to derail Winger's capturing her prey.

***Christopher Strong*** (1933). Directed by Dorothy Arzner. Arzner used to appear on sets in full men's drag and was a prolific Hollywood director, now a cult figure among cinematically inclined dykes. Check out this film where yet another cult favorite, Katharine Hepburn, plays a butch aviatrix.

***Deadly Weapons*** (1970). Directed by Doris Wishman. The only woman ever to direct exploitation flicks, Wishman hooked up with burlesque queen Chesty Morgan for two movies featuring her seventy-three-inch chest as first a murder weapon (*Deadly Weapons*) and then as a hiding place for her spy camera (*Double Agent 73*). Also check out *Taste of Flesh* by Wishman. This 1967 flick includes a romantic yet bizarre lesbian seduction scene that's so campy you have to see it to believe it.

**Entre Nous** (1983). Directed by Diane Kurys. Isabelle Huppert and Miou Miou star in this beautiful film about the intense emotional bond between two women. Added bonus: endless hours of debate that will ensue as to whether the two women are lesbians or not.

**Foxes** (1980). Directed by Adrian Lyne. Jodie Foster and Cherrie Currie (former lead singer of the Runaways) share some intense chemistry as the stars of this saga about teens grown up so fast that they seem more like "short forty year olds" than just your average fucked-up Valley teens trying to make it through their last year in high school. Extra trash appeal: stars Chachi (Scott Baio) as a skater kid.

**Lair of the White Worm** (1988). Directed by Ken Russell. Amanda Donohoe stars as a bloodthirsty, dildo wielding, giant, pagan goddess with a penchant for fair maidens and men alike. Camp thriller that cannot be missed!

**Lianna** (1983). Directed by John Sayles. A cult classic about a woman who, unfulfilled by her life as mother, wife and professional, turns to dyke bars where she finally finds what she's been missing and acknowledges that she's a lesbian.

**Liquid Sky** (1983). Directed by Slava Tsukerman. Anne Carlisle embodies the ultimate in polymorphous perversity by playing both a new-wave, bisexual girl and boy in this flick. Her female character bonds with a space alien who sucks the life out of every person she beds by killing them during their orgasm. Bad, low budget effects only offer more fun.

**Morocco** (1930). Directed by Josef von Sternberg. Marlene Dietrich raises blasé exoticism to an art form as a well-worn cabaret singer and Gary Cooper plays the man who falls for her. Includes the legendary scene where Dietrich, dressed in a tux, kisses a surprised female member of her audience.

**Ms. 45** (1981) and **Fear City** (1985). Directed by Abel Ferrara. Scum master Abel Ferrara loves lesbians, junkies, and prostitutes, which makes him either a genius or just a lower-budget Howard Stern. In *Ms. 45* Ferrara collaborator Zoe Tamerlis stars as a mute woman turned avenger, when she murders her rapist and then broadens her scope, so to speak. In *Fear City* Ferrara tells the story of two lesbian junkie strippers stalked by a murderer. By the end of the film, only one lesbian junkie stripper is left. Melanie Griffith plays the survivor and eventually falls for Tom Berenger. Yeah, it's messed up, but hey what do you want, how many movies about junkie dyke strippers are there anyway? Continuing with the lesbian junkie subtext, witness Annabella Sciorra giving Lili Taylor the massive hickey that turns her into a grad student of the night in his latest film, *The Addiction*.

**Personal Best** (1982). Directed by Robert Towne. Another cult classic of lesbian cinema. Mariel Hemingway and Patrice Donnelly star in this film about two track stars whose relationship is thwarted by a domineering coach (Scott Glenn).

**Poison Ivy** (1992). Directed by Katt Shea Ruben. Sara Gilbert and Drew Barrymore star in this trashy psychothriller about a budding femme fatale (Barrymore) who latches onto the lonely, alienated Cooper (Gilbert) and tries to become all things to Cooper and her father (Tom Skerritt). Bad film made fun by outstanding performance by Barrymore.

**Queen Christina** (1933). Directed by Rouben Mamoulian. Arguably one of Garbo's best films. It stars the great Garbo as a cavalier and gallant cross-dressing monarch. A favorite of film-theory eggheads.

**Two Moon Junction** (1988). Directed by Zalman King. Bad film about a southern deb (Sherilyn Fenn) who leaves the safety of her family to take up with a strapping carnival worker, but it includes a steamy scene where Fenn slow dances with Kristy McNichol.

---

## FIVE LESBIAN ROLE MODELS FROM SATURDAY MORNING CARTOONS:

1. Velma, from "Scooby Doo" (the bookish variety)
2. Alexandra, from "Josie and the Pussycats" (the Susan Sontag lookalike)
3. Isis, from "The Mighty Isis" (who wouldn't want super powers and a cool uniform?)
4. Natasha, from "Bullwinkle" (foreign accent, long legs, and all the brains in the outfit)
5. Wonder Woman (duh!)

---

# Dyke-themed Films

Here is an abridged listing of some of the most well-known and easily accessible mainstream films with lesbian themes or characters, all of which are available at most chain video stores.

*Bargirls* (1985). Intersecting stories of love, lust, dating, and heartache center around a lesbian bar that smacks of contrivance, yet manages to deliver humor, tenderness, and the curious straight friend that every queer girl has.

*Before Stonewall* (1985). Directed by Greta Schiller and Robert Rosenberg. A treat of a documentary about gay and lesbian life before the Stonewall uprising.

*Chanel Solitaire* (1981). Directed by George Kaczender. A bio pic about French fashion maven Coco that includes a sympathetic look at her lesbian relationship with Misia Cert.

*Claire of the Moon* (1992). Directed by Nicole Cann. A writer's workshop is the backdrop of this romantic flick about two pre-viously straight women who meet at the workshop and end up in bed together. Condemned by some as "boring," "slow," and downright "bad," it was the talk of the lesbian bars for weeks.

*Club des Femmes* (1936). Directed by Jacques Deval. A French film about an all-women's club where men are barred and one night club diva rules the roost.

*Desert Hearts* (1985). Directed by Donna Deitch. In this film adaptation of the dyke pulp-fiction classic, *Desert of the Heart,* Patrice Charbonneau plays a gorgeous butch dude-ranch resident who takes up with Helen Shaver, a literature professor in town for a quickie divorce.

*Forbidden Love* (1993). Directed by Lynne Fernie and Aerlyn Weissman. A Canadian documentary about lesbian life in the fifties mixed with dramatic vignettes taken from lesbian pulp fiction available at the time. Funny, sad, informative, and sexy, it's the *Paris Is Burning* of lesbian documentaries.

*Heavenly Creatures* (1994). Directed by Peter Jackson. In this New Zealand film about two young teens, Pauline and Juliet, who murder Pauline's mother, the line between fiction and reality continually blurs. Pauline and Juliet meet in school, fall in love, and then begin to create their own world in which they alone dwell. When Juliet's parents decide to send her to South Africa the girls devise a plot to stay together that involves a sort of *uebermenschian* killing of Pauline's wretched mother. The entire film is a dramatized version of a real event.

***Henry and June*** (1990). Directed by Philip Kaufman. Perhaps best watched without sound as Uma Thurman displays a clunky accent, yet manages to smolder as June to Maria de Medeiros's Anaïs. All right, so Henry Miller isn't exactly the most sensitive of men, but the heavy-lidded stares of Uma will send chills down your spine.

***Hotel New Hampshire*** (1984). Directed by Tony Richardson. Quirky adaptation of John Irving's saga of an eccentric family marred by incest, terrorism, and death. Highlights include Jodie Foster as a young woman exploring her sexuality, who temporarily ends up in bed with Nastassja Kinski.

***The Hunger*** (1983). Directed by Tony Scott. To many lesbians *The Hunger*, which features an almost baroque love scene between Catherine Deneuve and Susan Sarandon, is like the *Mona Lisa,* a perfect artwork to which they return again and again. Even Camille Paglia likes the movie and she's barely a lesbian. Basically a gothic thriller about vampires and sleep deprivation research. And if you can figure out what premise links the two, you'll love the film for more than the sex. Also stars David Bowie, with Ann Magnuson as the first onscreen victim.

***The Incredibly True Story of Two Girls in Love*** (1995). Directed by Maria Maggenti. Two girls, one working class and white, the other upper middle class and Afro-American, fall in love in a high school somewhere in Maryland. This incredibly cute, giggly, and autobiographical story is the feel-good lesbian movie of the century.

***Inside Monkey Zetterland*** (1992). Directed by Jeffery Levy. A bizarre, whimsical, directionless, yet entertaining satire about a former child actor, Monkey Zetterland (Steve Antin), who lives with his mother and supports himself on residual checks from TV movies. His dysfunctional family includes a lesbian sister Grace (Patricia Arquette) who returns to the family home and gets mixed up with the "outing" terrorists Sasha (Rupert Everett) and Sophie (Martha Plimpton). In the end, Grace is killed while planting a bomb in an insurance company's office, but is turned into a lesbian martyr.

***I've Heard the Mermaids Singing*** (1987). Directed by Patricia Rozema. A Canadian film about Polly, a temp at a Toronto art gallery who develops a crush on the worldly and sophisticated woman who is the gallery's owner.

***Je Tu Il Elle*** (1974). Directed by Chantal Akerman. For a slightly more palatable version of Franco-sapphic love see this movie about a young woman in search of herself. On the road to me-ville, she has a lesbian encounter and the dyke sex scene lasts nearly twenty minutes. Not as lively as *Les Biches,* but not everything can end in a cat fight to the death.

***Kamikaze Hearts*** (1991). Directed by Juliet Bashore. For a real-life saga of lesbian junkie strippers, check out this dark, sexy, dramatic documentary about a relationship between two women and their drug habits who just happen to work in the porn industry. Is real life stranger than fiction? In this case, yes.

***Les Biches*** (1968). Directed by Claude Chabrol. The late, great Vito Russo referred to this film as the only lesbian zipper fuck on celluloid. *Les Biches* is the story of a refined, wealthy woman who takes in a street teen as her lover. Eventually, a man comes between them and the street girl kills the woman who took her in, not before a great cat fight. The French are so progressive!

***Lilith*** (1964). Directed by Robert Rossen. A lyrical film about a woman, played to perfection by Jean Seberg, who finds comfort in the arms of another woman while institutionalized in a mental hospital.

***Mädchen in Uniform*** (1931). Directed by Leontine Sagan. In this early German film a young girl is sent to a militaristic boarding school where she develops a crush on a teacher who treats her kindly. The student is pushed toward the brink of suicide after the teacher is reprimanded for favoring her. A controversial film at the time it was made, it was banned in the U.S. and Sagan was exiled by the Nazis.

***Pandora's Box*** (1928). Directed by G. W. Pabst. Louise Brooks oozes silent sex appeal and positions herself as the only femme fatale to die for. The scene where she dances with another woman is legendary and well worth having a VCR with slow motion.

***Salmonberries*** (1991). Directed by Percy Adlon. k. d. lang makes her film debut as a character of indeterminate gender. She finds comfort in the arms of a stern East German librarian who has escaped to Alaska after her lover is killed while trying to escape over the now-defunct Berlin Wall. Unfortunately, there's only one k. d. song, which is played over and over again. Fortunately, she's buck naked in one (short) scene.

**Silkwood** (1983). Directed by Mike Nichols. In a sort of side-dish role, Cher plays a sassy-lipped lesbian in this gripping film about the life of antinuke activist and martyr Karen Silkwood (played by Meryl Streep).

**Three of Hearts** (1993). Directed by Yurek Bogayevicz. Kelly Lynch, Sherilyn Fenn, and Billy Baldwin are likable leads in this otherwise superficial and dyke-sexless film about a lesbian who devises some elaborately improbable plots to win back her bisexual girlfriend. Of course this doesn't happen and depending on which version you rent she either leaves them both behind or goes off with Baldwin.

**Waiting for the Moon** (1987). Directed by Jill Godmilow. Linda Hunt delights as Alice B. Toklas in this made-for-PBS bio of the relationship between Alice and Gertrude Stein.

# "Feminist" Flicks, or the Cinema of the Strong Woman

While there is a dearth of strong lesbian characters in mainstream cinema, there is also a total lack of powerful, rebellious women regardless of sexuality. There are however a few notable high points in the history of the filmic girl rebel. What follows is a list of rebellious females who have won a place in the collective dyke psyche.

**Alien, Aliens, Alien³** (1979, 1986, 1991). Directed by Ridley Scott, James Cameron, and David Fincher, respectively. Idol of many a dyke, Sigourney Weaver rules the universe as Ripley in all three installments of the Alien story. *Alien* and *Aliens* are widely believed to be the best. *Alien³* is only for hard-core Weaver fans.

**Born in Flames** (1983). Directed by Lizzie Borden. Told in a pseudodocumentary tone, this film is set in New York sometime after a socialist revolution has swept the country. Rad women of all colors and classes come together in a coup and take over the state-run media hoping to bring about a second revolution that will make everything better. (Yeah, and if you only follow the yellow brick road . . . ) If the whole "come together" theme doesn't grab you, it is worth seeing if only for the pc revenge scene where women on bicycles corral a rapist on a street in TriBeCa.

151

**Fried Green Tomatoes** (1991). Directed by Jon Avnet. This film adaptation of Fannie Flagg's novel sidesteps the lesbian relationship between Idgie (Mary Stuart Masterson) and Ruth (Mary Louise Parker) that was very clear in the book. The movie still has four engaging Southern women finding their own way in life.

**Gas, Food, and Lodging** (1992). Directed by Allison Anders. Anders's charming debut feature about a single mother (Brooke Adams) who works as a waitress to support herself and her two daughters Trudi and Shade (Ione Skye and Fairuza Balk). Trudi rebels against her mother and ends up in a home for pregnant teens while Shade escapes into her obsession with the extravagant stars of Spanish-language cinema. With fine performances from all three actresses, *Gas, Food, and Lodging* is a quirky but entertaining flick and also one of the few films to really depict a woman's point of view about the stress and strains of single parent family life. Also look for Anders's second feature *Mi Vida Loca* (1994).

**The Gold Diggers** (1983). Directed by Sally Potter. In theoretical lingo *The Gold Diggers* is a feminist, deconstructionist musical about two female heroines who find each other in the maze of the masculinist cinematic gaze, but what it really comes down to is Julie Christie starring as a golden girl who gets carried off on a white horse by her knight in shining armor, a black, female clerical worker. Also check out Potter's second feature, *Orlando,* her visually lush adaptation of Virginia Woolf's novel that stars that darling of the Brit art cinema, Tilda Swinton.

**Julia** (1977). Directed by Fred Zinneman. Based on Lillian Hellman's *Pentimento,* it features Hellman (Jane Fonda) recounting her lifelong relationship with the fiercely independent and political Julia (Vanessa Redgrave). Julia devotes her life to fighting fascism in the thirties and a trip to Europe brings Hellman and Julia back together again.

**A Question of Silence** (1983). Directed by Marlene Gorris. A group of women kick a store owner to death because he terrorized women, but of course, the white, male, corporate world doesn't understand this. When a judge asks if they would have done the same thing to a woman, they break out into uncontrollable laughter. A deeply disturbing and controversial film. Also worth a view—Gorris's second film *Broken Mirrors* (1985).

---

***Terminator 2: Judgment Day*** (1991). Directed by James Cameron. Despite the presence of robo-Republican Schwarzenegger, there are those who see this as a feminist film about how Sarah (Linda Hamilton) battles evil, saves the universe from a fiery apocalypse, and looks *very* good working those arms in a tank top. Whether one buys this or not, Hamilton plays a fiercely independent, physically strong woman who shoots things up almost as good as Thelma and Louise.

***Thelma and Louise*** (1991). Directed by Ridley Scott. The first and only big-budget, feminist buddy movie. Thelma (Geena Davis) and Louise (Susan Sarandon) set off for a weekend in the country where Louise interrupts a man attempting to rape Thelma and shoots him outside a bar. Things get out of hand after this murder and only get worse when Thelma takes to knocking over convenience stores. The film is great cathartic fun, but it is crippled by the Hollywood rule that once you declare your love for another woman, you have to die.

***Welcome Home, Roxy Carmichael*** (1990). Directed by Jim Abrahams. A very underrated film about a "crazy" girl's crush on other women. Winona Ryder is fabulous as the wacko babydyke Dinky (who, of course, doesn't know that's what she is, but trust me . . . if there were to be a sequel, she'd be one).

# FILMS YOU'LL NEVER SEE:

***My So Called Life: The College Years.*** Angela finally figures out that her attraction to Jordan Catalano was actually based on the fact that he was so pretty. She starts hanging out with Ricky at the local gay bar, and finds true love with a female Hostess delivery truck driver by the name of Jess.

***Darlene Conner: The Real Story.*** After graduation, Darlene goes on to graduate school, hooks up with some queer theory types, starts dressing in leather, and ties up undergraduate girls for fun. Upon reaching full professorship, she settles down with the chairwoman of the English Department, gets cats, grows old, and makes prank calls to David up until her death.

***Free Ellen!: Behind the Scenes.*** The Committee to Free Ellen DeGeneres (Cotfed) makes a documentary about the struggles of a lesbian sitcom star to stop living a lie. The film is suppressed by Hollywood publicists, and a movement is born. Final liberation comes when the Committee takes over the Emmy Awards and symbolically frees a dozen doves into the audience.

# OF WIMMIN'S MUSIC

Pop and rock are the only realms of mass entertainment where one will find more than a handful of out and loud lesbians. Hell, with the successes of "women's music," lesbians even invented our own genre of pop. Even for those who are not music junkies, pop music has become one of the few meaningful forces in modern culture. It can explain the world or just provide a distraction from the pain of your latest breakup. Whether one is a folkie, punker, rocker, or rapper, by identifying with a particular kind of music, lesbians make complex political statements about style and art all in the simple purchase of a single CD. And you thought all you had to know about lesbian music was Melissa Etheridge!

The bond between lesbians and pop was cemented in the seventies when lesbian feminists banded together to form two women's music record labels. The performers signed to these labels carried on the tradition of political folk music of the sixties. For those not around for the heyday of women's music, think of it as Bikini Kill unplugged and mellowed by Prozac. The first women's music label, Olivia, was born in 1972. In keeping with the "C'mon, people get together and love one another" ethos of the commune, Olivia Records was run as a collective. Olivia artists frequently played in front of "women-only" audiences. The women-only attitude extended beyond performers and audiences to the hiring of female producers, engineers, and stage technicians. With the notorious boy's club attitude of most men in the record industry, Olivia gave women a chance to enter the music industry in positions that before were often closed to them. Many of the Olivia stars are still releasing albums and touring today: Records by Cris Williamson, Meg Cristian, Tret Fure, and June Millington can be found in the record bins at most local gay and lesbian bookstores.

## Women's Music Hit Parade

**1.** *Changer and the Changed* by Cris Williamson. Released in 1975, it ended up moving over a quarter of a million copies, making it the best-selling women's music album of all time. Girl rock encyclopedist Gillian Garr has pointed out how much *Changer* . . . bears an eerie similarity to Carole King's *Tapestry* (as if that were a good thing). With shiny, happy songs about sisterhood and waterfalls, what more could a newly woman-identified woman want?

2. "Ode to a Gym Teacher" from Meg Cristian's 1975 album *I Know You Know*. The classic babydyke crush set to bawdy rock'n'roll.

3. "Woman Loving Women" from Teresa Trull's *The Ways a Woman Can Be*. An "I Am Lesbian Hear Me Roar" folk-rock anthem.

4. *Imagine My Surprise*—Folksinger Holly Near's 1978 album in which she outs herself after entering into a relationship with PE-teacher fetishist Cristian. She formed her own label, Redwood Records, in 1973 to release anti-war songs. When her relationship with Cristian became a matter of public knowledge a minifeud developed between Olivia (the label for which Cristian recorded) and Redwood over how the feminist audience would be carved up between them. However, all was settled peacefully by the great goddess above and they all drank a ceremonial cup of herbal tea at the next full moon to celebrate. Near later wrote a book called *Fire in the Rain . . . Singer in the Storm* that chronicles her life as a latent lesbian, peacenik, folk heroine.

5. *Lavender Jane Loves Lesbians*—What does Lavender Jane have in common with Slim Whitman? Both Alix Dobkin's first album and Mr. Whitman have been the butt of David Letterman jokes. Thus Dobkin holds the distinction of having been the only women's music album ever featured in a routine on "Late Night."

In the early seventies women's folk and women's music festivals began to spring up across the country. These festivals fostered a sense of unity among the lesbians who attended as well as offering a captive audience to whom the then-infant labels could market their wares. The Michigan Womyn's Music Festival emerged as the largest regular gathering of fans of music by women.

Unfortunately, the relationship between pop and politics is not always a quiet one and the Michigan Womyn's Music Festival has become the battleground for skirmishes between lesbians over everything from S/M to perfume. A gathering of thousands of lesbians should be an event that no self-respecting dyke should miss, and here's why.

## Top Ten Reasons to Attend a Womyn's Music Festival (At Least Once)

**10.** Expand your culinary horizons by trading tofu recipes in the mess tent.

**9.** Annoying sniffers by wearing a garlic necklace can be fun (added bonus: Keeps all those pesky lesbian vampires away).

**8.** Won't have to search all over for good vegetarian cuisine.

**7.** Can check out the latest trends in lesbian handicrafts and add to your labrys jewelry collection.

**6.** Satisfy your curiosity about whether women musicians have groupies or not.

**5.** Pick up lots of tips on new ways to wear flannel.

**4.** Unlike Woodstock where there were always long lines for the toilet, you know that the facilities will be available during the Cris Williamson set.

**3.** Where else can a lesbian vacation with so many other dykes and still have clothing be optional?

**2.** Lots of different lesbians from all over the country stuck in one place overnight = amazing odds that for once you will not know your one-night stand.

**1.** Topless dykes fill mosh pit during Tribe 8 show.

Many of the staples of contemporary adult-oriented rock like Melissa Etheridge, Tracy Chapman, Cindy Lee Berryhill, Tori Amos, Sarah McLachlan, Sophie B. Hawkins, Michelle Shocked, Suzanne Vega, and Natalie Merchant have perhaps unconsciously followed a path blazed by women's music performers and their success certainly came on the backs of Olivia and Redwood wimmin. Today, lesbian performers make mega bucks on major labels with videos in high rotation on VH1.

## The Big Four

### 1. Melissa Etheridge

Possessed of a middle-American warmth and a fiery, gut-wrenching voice, Melissa Etheridge was catapulted into the Top 40 by her Janis Joplin set at Woodstock '95 and since this performance (and not-to-be-forgotten coming out), has become the darling of the adult-oriented rocker set.

### 2. k.d. lang

This Canadian butch goddess (immortalized in the words of Madonna: "I've seen Elvis—and she's gorgeous!") rumbled around the CW scene before releasing her fifth album and first noncountry album of innovative and original torch songs, *Ingenue*, in 1992. Perhaps her most interesting phase though, was the I'm-Patsy-Cline-reincarnated stage when she and her band were called the Reclines (they released one album in 1984 called *A Truly Western Experience*, which contains the killer cut "Bopalena"). Her first album as k.d., and not the Reclines, is 1987's cheery, but mostly lukewarm *Angel with a Lariat*.

### 3. The Indigo Girls

These two Georgia girls, Amy Ray and Emily Saliers, are perhaps the best songwriters of all the big-time lesbian pop singers. While k.d. is easily the most strange, this duo represents lang's direct opposite—artistic and innovative, yet without pretension, they produce quality albums and tour exhaustively to bring their music to their fans. Following on the strength of *Strange Fire* (1987), the Indigo Girls were courted and signed by Epic, and won a Grammy for Best Folk Recording (1989).

### 4. Sophie B. Hawkins

Emerging as a scraggly haired pop angel in a flannel shirt in the "Damn, I Wish I Was Your Lover" video, Sophie B. Hawkins won the hearts of many a pop-loving dyke for her *Tongues and Tails* album. With friends as varied as transgender lesbian Kate Bornstein and Rosie O'Donnell, Hawkins maintains a free-spirited, independent persona. When asked if she was a lesbian by an interviewer, she admitted affairs with men, women, and a transgendered person and then concluded she was "omnisexual." Her 1995 *Whaler* album is pure, simple, dance pop that is both catchy and pretty.

## Alternadykes

Moving a bit to the left of the center from the Big Four and entering into the land of the alternative nation, one finds a number of dykes making happy homes. Kate Schellenbach, the improbable former drummer of the Beastie Boys, now in the all-girl funk/rock Luscious Jackson, is an out, proud dyke who was known to be dating the only nonbreeder

BETTMANN ARCHIVES

**k. d. lang,** fabulous song-stylist and lust object of girls worldwide, is one of the most famous "out" lesbian entertainers, and it hasn't hurt her career a bit. (Seen here holding her 1993 Juno Award—why . . . what did you think it was?)

Breeder, Brit bassist Josephine Wiggs. Topping the list of desirable alternadykes is Hole drummer, babydyke heartthrob Patty Schemel, who is not only an amazing drummer, but a lesbian style-plate and, unlike the other two, shares the alternadyke passion for hair dye.

# Dyke-Punk Bands

Far, far to the left of the glitzy MTV alternascene, is the burgeoning, queer punk scene ruled as it is by two killer all-dyke bands, Tribe 8 and Team Dresch. Without the backing of major labels and spurred on by the DIY punk attitude, dyke-punk bands are gathering the attention of the pop underground as well as mainstream outlets. There are a myriad of queer girl bands like New York's Kickstand, the late, great Boston band Tattle Tale, Seattle's Juned, San Francisco's Sta-Priest, or Portland's Third Sex, but here's the scoop on four of the most accessible dyke-punk bands traveling the current scene.

## Tribe 8

You gotta love this band who called their 1994 tour the Tits & Tofu Tour. Tribe 8 is a five-member multiethnic, all-dyke punk band from San Francisco who are known for their outrageous stage shows during which the lead singer, Lynn Breedlove, often wears a strap-on dildo. She has invited members of the audience on stage to suck her cock and has chopped the dildo in half while cursing out rapists. When they played the Michigan Womyn's Music Festival, they created, guess what, a huge stink about their act. Protesters offered special counseling to women who were upset by the band. Tribe 8 makes pointed attacks on the pc lesbian camp. On their song, "Manipulate," Breedlove taunts "Women's love its so friendly, women's love like herbal tea, women's love it empowers me." On "Lesbophobia" a song from their *By the Time We Get to Colorado* EP, Breedlove throws sisterhood out the window yet another time when she disses a straight woman who acts like an ass because she's afraid she's just been cruised by a girl. On "Neanderthal Dyke" Breedlove says "My political consciousness is fried/and I'm not exactly woman-identified/I don't give a shit I just want to get laid/by curvy little hot and sexy eyeliner babes."

## Team Dresch

No, it's not a softball team! Team Dresch is an indie-rock super group made up of four vegan dykes: punk heartthrob-bassist extraordinaire Donna Dresch who has played in many many bands over the last ten years; guitarist Jody Bleyle who is also the drummer-vocalist for the Portland band Hazel; singer Kaia is from Adickdid and a powerful solo performer in her own right; and drummer Marci Martinez was in the late, great Olympia band Calamity Jane. If those credentials weren't enough, two of the members, Jody and Donna have their own labels (Candy Ass and Chainsaw respectively) and have produced records for other bands. Their years of experience have not jaded Team Dresch, they are not looking for stardom, they are committed to being out and doing for themselves what the mainstream would never even care to do, producing quality punk rock about their being dykes. After Jody and Donna were queer-bashed following a show, they were inspired to bring Alice the Self-Defense Girl on their first tour to give self-defense lessons to their audience so that none of their fans will have to experience the same terror they did. Kaia's voice comes close to the smoldering sex appeal of Chrissie Hynde on early Pretenders songs and drenches her words in emotion with a style that is as free and careless in enunciation as was early Michael Stipe. Hers is the voice that you have always wanted to hear sing a dyke love song, but never dreamed you ever would.

## Come

While not a punk band like Tribe 8 and Team Dresch, this Boston-based, guitar-heavy blues band blends swirling guitar sounds and the occasional classic rock riff with the ragged emotionalism of vocalist-guitarist Thalia Zedek's raspy voice. On Come's second LP *Don't Ask, Don't Tell,* Zedek's haunted tones speak poetically and politically about dyke desire and loss.

## Fifth Column

This group of Canadian punks fronted by artist/filmmaker/actress/zine star G. B. Jones have released five LPs over the last several years. On their most recent release, *36C,* Fifth Column sounds like what the Cramps would be if they were a dyke band.

# Dyke Folk Music

One wonders if Joan Baez ever imagined that a figure like Ani di Franco or Phranc would be the successors to her throne as the queen of folk, oh those years ago. They are not gentle waiflike folkies, but rather in your face, punk folksingers with a bad attitude and booming voices to shout it in. Folk continues to be a favorite genre of dykes who are drawn not only to the new breed of folksingers like Phranc or Ani, but continue to support women's music type folkies like Nanci Griffith, Toshi Reagon, Castlebury & DuPree, and Das Fallopia.

## Ani di Franco

The most visceral new folk, or punk folkie around is Ani di Franco. Her edgy voice rips through poetic meditations about relationships with boys and girls, political rants, and evocative portraits of everyday life. With wild guitar arrangements that alternate between plugged and un-plugged, she is truly one of the most innovative of the neo-folkies. She has numerous albums out, but her best yet is 1994's *Out of Range.*

## disappear fear

The D.C. duo of Sonia Rutstein and Cindy Frank, known as disappear fear, weave political lyrics about apathy, gay bashing, and racism with pleasing harmonies. With a cheery, bouncy, vocal style not unlike Natalie Merchant, disappear fear tackles issues in a sincere and honest manner, yet with some fierce guitar playing and a hot groove, they have a huge appeal.

## Phranc

Jewish lesbian folksinger Phranc is also a die-hard punk who was part of the LA hard-core scene and opened for the Smiths in the eighties. She put out numerous LPs, did a one-woman show about her obsession with Neil Diamond, and gave us such classics as "I Don't Like Female Mud Wrestling" or "The Caped Crusader" about the pope. Phranc's recent single "Bulldagger Swagger" is an acoustic ditty about the trials and tribulations of being a "very very butch lesbian" trying to use a women's bathroom. Released by the punk label Kill Rock Stars, her latest release *Goofyfoot* emphasized her place in the punk world for a whole new generation not familiar with her earlier work.

## Ferron

The lesbian answer to Morrisey's whining, ultra unhappiness is Ferron, the gin-sodden antidote to militantly cheerful folksingers. Her songs are resolutely unhappy and forever mopey. More than resembling Morrisey or redoing Dylan, she is the lesbian Leonard Cohen and thank god someone is.

# Rocker Girls

The pop-rock world divides up into two groups where lesbians are concerned. Basically, it goes like this, there is music made by lesbians and music listened to by lesbians. Lesbians, more than any other group, listen to and buy music made by women artists. While we may enjoy boy rock and pop, what really rocks our world are, of course, women performers straight or queer. Often we find ourselves attracted to the more offbeat women artists out there and lesbians are among the strongest supporters of performers like Diamanda Galas, Tori Amos, Me'Shell N'Dege-Ocello, Annie Lennox, Sarah McLachlan, Kate Bush, Jane Sieberry, the Cocteau Twins, and Dead Can Dance to name just a few. On the other hand, Sheryl Crow and Veruca Salt claim to have a big lesbian following, so that just goes to show that there's no accounting for some dyke taste.

On the rocker girl side, dykes have always revered unconventional figures like Patti Smith, Bonnie Raitt, Joan Armatrading, or Joni Mitchell, raising them to virtual cult figures within the dyke community. Many younger dykes have also extended membership in the mothers of invention cult to such punk heroines as Poly Styrene (of X-Ray Spex), the Raincoats, the Slits, Siouxsie Sioux, Exene Cervenka, and the Go Go's.

On the current rocker-girl scene, lesbians split their loyalties between the adult alternative artists mentioned above, alternarockers like Hole, Babes in Toyland, and L7 (who aren't really alternative) and riot grrrl bands like Bikini Kill. Of these three groups, the alternagirl bands and the riot grrrl bands are the most politically active and supportive of dyke concerns. By bending the mainstream to make room for loud, nasty, feminist girls, alternative bands and riot grrrl bands should be important facets of every pop-loving dyke's life.

## Rocker Girl:

Courtney Love is her heroine and she follows one of the many bands that feature women as more than a pretty backup singer or girlfriend/model. Some may be misled by the babydoll dresses and the makeup, but don't be confused. The rocker woman, or "alternadyke," can fight the power with the best of the "androgyny is the way to women's liberation" set.

# Riot Grrrl

Riot grrrls are young feminist activists who militate around issues like sexual abuse and abortion rights and encourage other girls to speak up and make noises about oppression and victimization. While many riot grrrls are not lesbians, they are the nineties equivalent of radical feminists. Riot grrrl shows, like women's music concerts, often include elements that "empower" girls, for instance making the pit area (an often de facto boy-only space) a girl-only place or through lyrics that encourage rebellion against stereotypical girl behavior. For those who strain to understand the youngsters today, or for those rad lezzies of the seventies who think the young women today are apathetic losers, here's a quick comparison card between Womyn and Grrrls.

## Womyn v. Grrrl

| Womyn | Grrrl |
|---|---|
| believes that going topless is a sign of empowerment | believes that going topless is a sign of empowerment only if accompanied by magic marker spelling out DYKE or SLUT scrawled across belly or chest |
| wants a loom | wants a distortion pedal for guitar |
| volunteers at battered women's shelter | writes a song about O.J. and Nicole and spousal abuse or in support of Lorena Bobbit |
| makes Venus of Willendorf sculptures | publishes a zine called Pussy Assassins |
| leads the fight for a women's center | pushes the boys out of the girl-only mosh pit at the Bikini Kill show |
| wears labrys jewelry | wears labrys tattoos |
| has a portrait of Sojourner Truth | has a portrait of Yoko Ono |
| supports No Nukes | supports Free Aileen Wurnos |
| vegetarian | vegan |

Now that we know what a riot grrrl is, sort of, here's what she's likely to listen to:

## Bikini Kill

Their first release was a homemade cassette called *Revolution Girl Style Now* and not long after Bikini Kill was made into the most visible manifestation of the riot grrrl movement. A media frenzy made them into the next great thing, despite their own claims that they are not exactly riot grrrls, didn't care about being on a major label, and didn't want to be rock stars. Vocalist Kathleen Hanna chants in "Rebel Girl": "When she talks, i hear the revolution/in her hips, there's revolutions/when she walks, the revolution's coming/in her kiss i taste the revolution."

## Heavens to Betsy/Sleater–Kinney

Known as H2B, the group is made up of two girls, Corin Tucker and Tracy Sawyer. They each switch off instruments to produce intense, emotion-filled songs of love and hate. With gender-inclusive lyrics H2B offer sincere lyrics about living through dysfunctional love stories for straight and queer alike. H2B have one LP out called *Calculated* on Kill Rock Stars and many singles but the best is "Direction" released in 1994 on Chainsaw. Shortly after this release, H2B broke up and Corin formed the world's first rock-inspired grrrl band called Sleater–Kinney and put out a self-titled EP in 1995 on villa villakula.

## Bratmobile

One of the earliest Olympia grrrl bands, Bratmobile is gone now, but never forgotten. With an exuberant pop-laden brand of girl punk, their only full length recording, the aptly titled *Pottymouth*, contains a cover of the Runaways "Cherry Bomb" as well as such ditties as "Fuck Yer Fans," "Cool Schmool," and the all-time fave "Panik" about a girl who's the "Joanest Jett around."

## Huggy Bear

This mixed group of Brit boys and girls are the vanguard of English queer punk. They cite Situationists in the liner notes to their 1993 full-length disc *Taking the Rough with the Smooch*, rant against queerphobia, and produce raging noise punk especially on "Shaved Pussy Poetry," "Herjazz," and "Derwin."

## Free Kitten

In 1990 on a promo disc for the Sonic Youth's first record on a major label, Kim Gordon, that group's bassist-vocalist, said "Women being outside of the male-structured world do make for more natural anarchists. [Therefore] girls invented punk rock, not England, not the United States, girls." Two years later she backed this up by covering "Oh Bondage Up Yours" with her band Free Kitten. On this single, Free Kitten is Gordon, Julie Cafritz (from Pussy Galore), and Yoshimi (the drummer for the Japanese noise band the Boredoms). At other times Free Kitten includes just Gordon and Cafritz or expands to include Yoshimi and Mark Ibold the bassist from Pavement. Their first full-length release was 1995's *Nice Ass*.

## Alternarocker Girls

### Hole

Led by the inimitable and infamous Courtney Love, Hole (guitarist Eric Erlandson, bassist Melissa Auf Der Mar, and drummer Patty Schemel) is much more interesting than anything that can ever be written about them. *Pretty on the Inside,* Hole's first album, coproduced by Kim Gordon is a powerful, deeply disturbing work of pure genius. On cuts like "Babydoll," "Mrs. Jones," and "Teenage Whore," Love's screeching vocals carry the instrumental miasma on her back. To some she is a modern-day prophet of what it is to be a woman living on the edge, to others she is a crass and materialistic manipulator, but whatever, she is one of the most intriguing female figures in mainstream rock. Proudly displaying her dyke drummer who plays each gig with a big DYKE sticker on her bass drum and an admittedly feminist outlook, Love has no predecessors in the ground that she charts.

### The Gits

Fronted by Mia Zapata, the Gits replayed California hard core with a grunge inflection. At her best on cuts like "Another Shot of Whiskey," "Here's to Your Fuck," or "Second Skin," Zapata's bluesy lyrics delivered in a rapid-fire punk style are devastating. Instrumental in the Seattle scene, Zapata was raped and murdered. More than a year after her death, her murder remains unsolved. Though the Gits second album remained unfinished at the time of Zapata's death, her bandmates sorted through the prep material and released *Entering the Conquering Chicken* as a posthumous tribute, which was followed by *Evil Stig* (Gits Live backwards), the Joan Jett–fronted tribute to Zapata.

## Babes in Toyland

Founded in the late eighties, Babes in Toyland is composed of guitartist-vocalist Kat Bjelland, drummer Lori Barbero, and bassist Maureen Herman. Bjelland's voice is visceral and acidic. As she shreds her way through a song, her voice burns with fury as she snaps and snarls lines like "My name is Gretel yeah I've got a crotch that talks" on Fontanelle's "Handsome & Gretel." At other moments, she may be more introspective, but no less relentless or forgiving as on "Lashes" where she cries "I put on my best Sunday dress and I waltz into this mess of mine posing as a guest or something much else than a crazy old doll in a crazy old dress."

## PJ Harvey

Polly Jean and her band offer a sound that is at once a continuation of the ground mapped out by the singer-songwriters of the seventies and a reinterpretation of this tradition. Taking the wounded poetics of an artist like Joni Mitchell, she blends them with a sort of frank, but slightly tortured sexuality. PJ Harvey is assertive yet vulnerable, introspective yet in the end she is painfully extroverted. PJ is an excellent guitarist, yet her sound is not about any other instrument but her voice.

## L7

L7 is made up of Donita Sparks (guitarist-vocalist), Jennifer Finch (bassist-vocalist), Suzi Gardner (guitarist), and Dee Plakas (drummer grrrl) and they are first of all rock entertainers, then secondly an all-girl band that can really rock. They do witty songs about trash cinema heroine Ms. 45, skinhead Jesus freaks, and the variety of Mr. Integrity types who roam the pop landscape. They are the founders of Rock for Choice, which has put on a number of benefit shows for the Fund for the Feminist Majority and speak out about issues related to reproductive freedom for women.

## 7 Year Bitch

Searing guitars and a powerful bass propel this all-girl, part-dyke band as lead singer, Selene Vigil, spews out political lyrics like "Dead Men Don't Rape" or "I Want a Fucking Riot." Though 7 Year Bitch's lyrics reveal them to be the most overtly political of the more mainstream bands, they are not solely an agitpop band. Vigil's lyrics span the range from the politics of rape to surviving life on the edge, as she cries out about living through a life crammed with one-too-many cigarettes and a few-too-many beers on "Tired of Nothing" and laments drug addictions like the one that brought band member Stefanie Sargent to a fatal heroin overdose on "Hip Like Junk."

## Resources

So now that you know the score, here's where you can follow your favorite bands or write away for their latest release.

### Zines/Magazines

Ben is Dead, PO Box 3166, Hollywood, CA 90028
Hot Wire Magazine: The Journal of Women's Music & Culture, 510 N. Wayne, Chicago, IL 60640 (312) 769-9009
Option, 1522-B Cloverfield Blvd., Santa Monica, CA 90404
Rockrgrl, 7W. 41st Ave. #113, San Mateo, CA 94403 Email: rockrgrl@rockrgrl.com

### Labels

Chainsaw Records Dept. A, PO Box 42600, Portland, OR 97242
Dischord Records, 3819 Beecher St. NW, Washington, D.C. 20007
K Records, PO Box 7154, Olympia, WA 98507
Kill Rock Stars, 120 N.E. State Ave. Suite 418, Olympia, WA 98501
Outpunk, PO Box 170501, San Francisco, CA 94117
Righteous Babe Records, PO Box 95, Ellicott Station, Buffalo, NY 14205 (Ani di Franco's label)

Simple Machines, PO Box 10290, Arlington, VA
22210–1290
villa villakula, PO Box 730, New York, NY 10009

## Mail Order Services

LadySlipper Catalog
(800) 634–6044

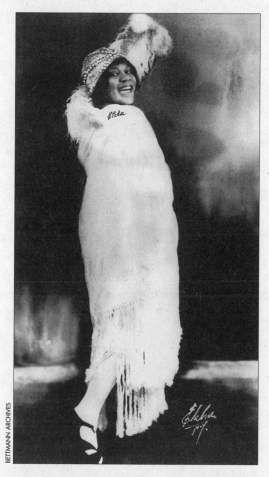

**Bessie Smith,** not only a great lesbian icon for her many classic blues songs about how love will break your heart (Sing it, Girl!) but quite a hot number herself.

# Miscellaneous
# for the Advanced
# Lesbian

# BAD JOKES

These bad jokes are provided as a public service. We do not condone their use or repetition. They are presented here only as a way to expose them and we hope squash them. Read at your own risk.

## The Mother of All Bad Lesbian Jokes

**Q.** How many lesbians does it take to screw in a light bulb?
**A.** That's not funny.

## Variations

**Q.** How many lesbians does it take to screw in a light bulb?
**A.** Two. One to screw it in and another to say "That's not funny."

**Q.** How many lesbian feminists does it take to screw in a light bulb?
**A.** Two. One to screw it in, and Andrea Dworkin to say "That's not funny."

**Q.** How many lesbians does it take to change a tire?
**A.** That depends on whether they're butch or femme.

## Butch Jokes (as told by femmes)

**Q.** How many femmes does it take to change a tire?
**A.** Two. And no help from AAA.

**Q.** How many butches does it take to change a tire?
**A.** Six. Two to change the tire and four to stand around drinking, chatting, and telling the two changing it how they're doing it all wrong.

**Q.** What do you call it when two butches have sex?
**A.** Banging tools.

**Q.** What do you call two butches bonding?
**A.** Monday night football.

**Q.** What's a butch's favorite place to stop?
**A.** The Snap-On Tools outlet.

## Femme Jokes (as told by butches)

**Q.** How many femmes does it take to change a tire?
**A.** Two. One to call AAA and the other to whine about the axle grease on her skirt.

**Q.** How many butches does it take to change a tire?
**A.** One. With no jack.

**Q.** What do you call two femmes having sex?
**A.** Bumping pocketbooks.

**Q.** What do you call two femmes bonding?
**A.** Expensive.

**Q.** What's a femme's favorite place to shop?
**A.** Anywhere.

## Miscellaneous Jokes

**Q.** What did one lesbian say to the other after they slept together for the first time?
**A.** "The moving truck's coming at ten."

## Skater/Grunge Girl:

Born on the west coast, this look picked up speed and made its way east. The obligatory items: tattoo (the temporary ones are not allowed), biker wallet, deliveryman jacket, and a thrift-store T-shirt from some unknown auto shop in Delaware. She also sports a rebellious attitude that can be worn either with or without a skateboard. The hat can be optional, depending on how greasy the hair (the cleaner it is, the more likely she'll wear the hat).

Every young dyklet has her icons: Barbara Stanwyck, Tura Satana, Janis Joplin to name a few. But we also have those real women we interact with every day, women in our cities and towns who make our hearts beat a little faster, with a mysterious allure that we don't fully understand at the time. In hindsight, they illustrate our futures with surprising clarity.

**Librarians:** Librarians are the perfect role models for the more intellectual young. They command great power—who else can shut up an entire room of rowdy children with just an icy stare over her glasses? The librarian is possessed of an iron fist in a velvet glove, and if you don't believe it, just try returning a book that's more than thirty days overdue. They've also got what you want—knowledge. They control it, they know how and where to find it, and if you ask nicely, they might let you get a look at it. The role of librarian is best dealt with by supplication, submission, and humility. There's a certain element of domination inherent in being a librarian that most philistines don't pick up, but those who do are the better (and more satisfied) for it.

**Teachers:** For the budding lesbian, women with power are not just role models, but a bit of a turn on as well. How many stories have we read of young women with school-girl crushes on their teacher? There's a reason for the cliché: As with librarians, they're smart, they're hot and they can boss people around. We yearn for furtive moments in the book closet or locker room, all heaving bosoms and loosened garments.

The most popular teachers seem to be: English teachers, gym teachers and less frequently, Social Studies.[1] Math, science, and Home Ec teachers rarely attain role model status, unless they're "out" at school, in which case they'll be besieged by young women who want nothing more than to loll at their feet and gaze at them longingly.

---

[1] Oddly enough, the most frequent lesbian teaching couples consist of one English teacher and one gym teacher.

**Law Enforcement:** Now that most police forces have women on them, this category has seen a distinct rise. While most politically aware youngsters have problems with police in principle (and some in reality), the sight of a woman in uniform has been known to unlock stirrings previously hidden. For those in the Northwest, or who are squeamish about police, you can choose from a wide variety of Wildlife Preservation Officers in handsome forest green uniforms. Or, having seen Jodie Foster in *Silence of the Lambs,* maybe an FBI agent would be more your speed. Often, during lesbian and gay rights demonstrations, whole groups of women are distracted from their appointed missions (blocking a street, chanting, etc.) by one particularly hot female officer.

**Military:** Again, the same problems are inherent here as with police officers. But let's be honest, whatever your feelings about the Army, Navy, Air Force, Marines, Margerethe Cammemeyer **is** a sex symbol.

**Your Unmarried Aunt:** Most people have one aunt in their family who never married, lived an interesting life of independence (at least for the times, and often as a teacher), and may or may not have shared a home with a female "roommate." These women, whether or not lesbian, were a source of strength to those who grew up being told that their options were marriage or a lonely life. By knowing these women, we learned this was a crock. (If you have an aunt like this, be sure to thank her.)

**Nuns:** This may sound odd, but nuns, for Catholic women, are great role models. Many of them teach, and are independent of men (unless you firmly believe in the "marrying God" doctrine). The publication of *Breaking the Silence: Lesbian Nuns Speak Out* only confirmed what some had long suspected: It wasn't all self-flagellation and guilt behind the iron gates. While present-day society doesn't necessitate joining the convent to live in a community of women, for some it was the first inkling that a life without boys was possible.

Other less popular, or more quirky role models would include: school lunch ladies, postal workers, government officials, and transit workers. All in all, a young lesbian can simply look around herself and find a host of inspiration, without having to hop a plane to New York or San Francisco.

# BUTCH/FEMME

It may have started with Sappho and her girl-jocks. We don't know because we don't have pictures, and she didn't write any odes to her strong woman in a short skirt (the Greek equivalent of cross-dressing). But butch/femme still has a long history, and one which can't be ignored. (Good books on the topic are listed in the Resource Guide, p. 221.)

While the terms are defined in Terminology, (see p. 11), a more in-depth look is called for, as the roles have changed quite a bit in our recent past. Where once a butch would be vilified for wearing a dress, or pursuing another butch, now there's femme/femme relationships, butch cross-dressing in House Balls (see Jennie Livingston's *Paris Is Burning*) and an unofficial Butch/Femme Continuum, not unlike the Lesbian Continuum except it's not as obvious.

There are, in fact, five categories:

▼ Butch (This might be "stone" butch, or just plain out there about her role.)
▼ Femmy Butch (A little harder to call.)
▼ Butchy Femme (Again, a little harder to call.)
▼ Femme (You know her when you see her.)
▼ "I'm not into roles." (Often this is true. Sometimes this is about denial.)

To assess where a woman falls in the continuum, here's a handy checklist to help.

**1.** Does she change her own oil?
Butch, Femmy Butch, Butchy Femme.

**2.** Does she look like she'd rather die than wear a dress?
Butch.

**3.** Does she call you up when there's a large bug in her apartment?
Cannot assess. No one like bugs in their apartment.

**4.** Does she actually get a manicure?
Could be any.
Does she come back with French tips and ruby red nail polish?
Butchy Femme, Femme.

**5.** Is she on a first name basis with all the guys who work in her office building?
Butch, Femmy Butch (less likely).

**6.** Which sports does she play?
Softball: Butch, Femmy Butch, Butch in Denial.
Tennis: Femme, Butchy Femme, Femme in Denial.
Rugby: Butch. (You don't even have to ask anymore for this one.)
Golf: Femmy Butch, Butchy Femme.
Badminton: Femme.
Bowling: Any category.

**7.** If she and a friend are traveling by car, does she agonize when NOT driving?
Butch, Femmy Butch, Butchy Femme.

**8.** If she's in K-Mart, where does she gravitate?
Discount Cosmetics: Femme, Butchy Femme.
Work Clothes: Butch.
Appliances: Butchy Femme.

**9.** Is she a control queen?
Yes: Butch, Femme.
No: All others.

**10.** Does she try and dress you up in suits and ties when you go out?
Yes: Femme, Butchy Femme.
(Guess what that makes you.)

# WANNABEES

You all know them, you've seen them in bars or clubs or at Pride events. "Straight Queers." "Lesbian-identified straight women." Wannabees, as in "I wannabe a lesbian." Yeah, well, I wannabe Hillary Clinton's studpuppy, but we can't have everything, can we? Many are called, and few are chosen, to quote the Good Book (see Ten Myths Demystified, p. 7).

What's up with these chicks? Sure, it's cool to be a dyke. But let's get honest here: It's not all about cool clothes, hot sex, and getting your own parade. Reno, the hyperactive performance artist once did a routine that summed it up nicely: "Hey, great! I can join an oppressed minority, get no recognition, lose my job, my parents, my home, get killed on the street for kissing my lover, and have millions of people hate me for no reason at all? Sign me up!"

While "Lesbian Chic" may be the germ for "wannabee"-ism, or maybe "wannabees" invented "Lesbian Chic" to make themselves feel good, either way a lot of dykes have been pissed off about turning something both personal and political into one big marketing strategy.

## The Pros and Cons of "Wannabee"-ism

| Pros | Cons |
|---|---|
| *Visibility:* People see more of us, in both quantity and variety. | People in the closet are still in the closet. |
| *Sisterhood:* Building bonds and bridges between women. | They won't sleep with you. |
| *Political Enlightenment:* for "wannabees" and those around them. | They *still* won't sleep with you. |
| *Press:* Lots of trendy magazine pieces (with photos). | Will they stand and fight when the chips are down??? |

The difficulty is of course finding the balance—sure it's cool to be queer, but there are so many other issues that have to be dealt with. When ACT UP became "the thing to do" in the late eighties, many members were irate that the meetings were turning into a big cruising spot (and perhaps rightly so). What also came out of this, however, were people who came to cruise, and stayed to fight.

While a political movement is not parallel to sexual identity, the argument can be made that a visible lesbian presence in the "mainstream" media accomplishes two goals:

▼ Lesbian youth see adults like themselves and realize they're not alone.

▼ Straight people can't ignore our existence for however long we're on the television, or the movie screen, or the radio.

Unfortunately, a rise has been reported in straight women teasing incidents. You may be familiar with this yourself, gentle Reader. A woman you meet is indeterminate about her preference, begins to spend a great deal of time with you, talks about how close you two are getting, and then, just when you think she's ready to take the plunge, after much eye-contact and sighing, she ups and pulls heterosexuality out of her back pocket, and you never see her again. We all know this sucks. And no one wants to be led down the primrose path, only to be pushed ceremoniously into the nettles. So, caveat girlfriend. Just be careful, and don't expect too much from women who may or may not have chosen to call themselves "lesbian-identified straight women." A few words for them:

1. What the hell does that mean?

2. If you're bisexual, great. Come out as such and help create the burgeoning bi movement.

3. If you're really and truly straight, there's nothing we can do about it. Sorry.

4. If you're a lesbian, and you're just not ready to talk about it, don't worry. We probably already know.

5. Just because you've read all of Lillian Faderman's lesbian literature anthology doesn't mean that you're "les-

bian identified." It means you probably have more time than the average sister.

6. Be careful about giving your phone number out to the members of riot dyke bands. Someday they just might call you, and if you don't put out, they'll be pissed.

## FOUR FAMOUS WANNABEES

1. Madonna—The Mother of All Wannabees.
2. Roseanne.
3. Sharon Stone—Well, okay, perhaps she's a "Shouldbee."
4. Susan Sarandon—Really a "Don't you wish she was" but we'll take her any way we can get her.

# "HOW COME STRAIGHT GIRLS GET ALL THE MONEY?"

## OR
## HOW TO MEET RICH AND FAMOUS LESBIANS, AND MAKE THEM YOURS

It's no secret that many a mother has said to her pre-pubescent daughter, "Remember, dear, love is all well and good, but it won't pay the rental on your humble flat. . . ."[1] Most mothers intended this wisdom to apply to future male suitors, never thinking that their little girl with the frilly party dress and the absurd crush on the Bay City Rollers would ever become a lesbian. Later on, they would be forced to confront the specter of homosexuality in its many facets: Liberace wasn't just "creative," Kristy NcNichol never got out of her tomboy phase, and their daughter was "that way." However, in that infinite flexibility which future lesbians have in interpreting parental advice, some have grown up to become adults with the belief in partners with "means."[2]

This stated, our simple guide should assist those inclined to seek women with more money/more fame/a higher TVQ in their quest for fulfillment and happiness. Note that said quest is a difficult and lonely road, and some supportive anonymous counseling should be sought.

---

[1] Some mothers also broke into a rendition of "Diamonds Are a Girl's Best Friend" at this point.
[2] "Means" is a relative term. For some, it might simply be someone who can afford to eat out and see a movie once in a while.

# Rule #1

While "rich and famous" is a well-worn phrase for the reason that these two characteristics travel together frequently (rich people are famous, and *vice versa*), for lesbians this holds no water.

**Proof:**

    **a.** Women make 69¢ to a male $1.00.

    **b.** "Famous lesbian" is oxymoronic; a famous lesbian is rarely "known" as both. You will often find a "famous" closet case, or a "rich" lesbian with a lot of closets and a husband to boot.[3]

**Corollary:** If you find a "famous lesbian," she is probably making even less than the 69¢ mentioned in statement (a).

    **c.** Rich lesbians are few and far between. Those who are rich and "out" are usually *NOT* at the local girls' club,[4] watching sweaty go-go dancers.

**Quod erit demonstrandum:** You need a strategy, and well-picked targets.

# Rule #2

For either the rich (R) or famous (F) lesbian (L), having a marketable skill is a big plus. In recent times, hiding a lover as a secretary/hairdresser/personal assistant/road manager/gallery assistant has become a way to assure that the press will find a better way to refer to a significant other than "playmate," in addition to making sure you're always close at hand (so to speak).

    Some might find accepting a salary for "services performed" a bit too close to well . . . prostitution. One might rationalize this by saying "Well, it's better than having her pay for everything; I still have my autonomy." (It's also a tax write-off for the employer.) If this works for you, fine. Otherwise you might want to consider hiring someone to ac-

---

[3] One might refer to husbands in these situations as a "travel closet." Or perhaps a "removable beard."

[4] Or the Girls' Club, for that matter.

tually perform the work, paying them the salary, and escaping the issue altogether.

(*Note:* During an intimate moment, if a woman asks you if you can type, you have either "hit the jackpot," or found a personnel director with a job opening. Answer at your own risk.)

# Rule #3

Discretion is the key to a relationship of this kind; more than sex, more than love, more than shopping for Lalique.

If you were hoping to continue your "in your face" activism (or "in your lap" performance art) while seeing a well-known celebrity, you would be wise to pick something other than Dyke Action Machine! Perhaps PETA or Greenpeace might be able to use you. The odds of someone's publicist not frothing at the mouth when learning of your chaining yourself to Ron Labon[5] are about equal to Tiffany's opening their wedding registry to same-sex couples in the foreseeable future.

Another problem regarding discretion: when one meets someone, their instinct is to call everyone they know and share the good news (especially sharing at length with ex-girlfriends who have dumped one publically and/or painfully). When dating a R/FL, you cannot tell *anyone.* You'll have to lie to roommates: "Oh, I'm going to the store for a while . . . don't wait up."; your parents: "No, Mom, that's not me in that picture . . . what would I be doing at the MTV Awards?"; and your *close* friends: "Yes, I'm still single, but I can't sleep with you . . . really. I'm trying to explore celibacy. Stop laughing . . ."

# Rule #4

If you find yourself unhappy, isolated, alone with a lot of lovely clothes, some lingerie, and waiting by the phone, try consoling yourself with these two thoughts:

▼ Your mother also told you seeds that you swallowed would grow into plants in your stomach. . . .

[5] The man (using the term loosely) behind the Oregon Citizens Alliance and Proposition 9.

▼ Many more lawyers are willing to explore "galimony" suits these days. . . .

## Do's and Don'ts

▼ *Do* show off your knowledge of their life. Almost anyone is flattered by research.

▼ *Don't* become obsessive about it. The minute you start discussing what size their training bra was, you have become the subject of a Brian DePalma film.

▼ *Do* keep up with current events, or else you'll be mistaken as a trick.[6]

▼ *Don't* answer the phone when you're staying over (unless you are employed at that address). Liz Smith knows perfectly well when someone is pretending to be a plumber.

▼ *Do* offer to pay your own way when you can, especially in public. (This will contribute to dignity-maintenance and dispel those nasty rumors.)

▼ *Don't* write your names together in a big heart in the bathrooms of popular lesbian bars.

---

### FUN THINGS TO DO WITH YOUR FAMOUS GIRLFRIEND

▼ Dress up in drag and take her to the Academy Awards as her new boytoy Jake.

▼ Play footsie under the table while she's meeting with *Entertainment Weekly*.

▼ Answer the fan mail with photos of your latest hot tub encounter.

---

[6] For more on "tricks," see Fran Lebowitz, "Notes on Trick," *Metropolitan Life* (1981).

# RELIGION AND SPIRITUALITY

Despite recent trends to the contrary, The United States of America was founded on the principle of freedom of religion. With this in mind, we come to an exploration of lesbian spirituality.[1] You can find four common themes which run through most dyke spiritual practices:

1. *Lack of men:* Traditionally, men have run religion. This is a problem when you're trying to create a spiritual world around women. Guys tend toward making big sweeping pronouncements, finish everyone's sentences, drink all the sacred wine, and then make crude remarks about the female deities behind their backs. So, for the most part, lesbian spirituality privileges female thought and spirit.

2. *Historical input:* Instead of ignoring matriarchal cultures, or those which worshipped female goddesses, lesbians involved in spiritual movements tend to elevate them. Whether it's Gaia or Shiva (and who couldn't use a goddess of destruction every once in a while), dykes have put in quite a few hours at the library.

3. *Candles:* No one knows why, but candles seem to figure prominently in lesbian rituals, spiritual or otherwise. From potlucks to sex, from prayer to pro-choice rally, you'll always find girls toting candles. The Lesbian Avengers have taken this to a new level—by eating fire, they've turned themselves into a form of human candle.

4. *Touch:* Physical contact—holding hands, massage—figures into various manifestations of the spiritual dyke.

---

[1] "Religion," with its connotations of organization, houses of worship, and, often, homophobia, is discarded here for the broader term. Additionally, there is not an official "lesbian religion," as interesting an idea as that is.

There's even one theorist who insists that footwashing as done by the Christians was begun by "Spike," the lost 13th disciple of Jesus, who lived as a man and worked with Joseph in the carpentry shop. However, we'll never know, as once Spike died in a vicious masonry accident and his true gender was revealed, all mentions of her were expurgated from New Testament editions.

## LESBIAN HIGH HOLY DAYS

▼ Birth of St. Butch, the first female mechanic (worked on chariots in Rome, A.D. 67–137).

▼ Feast of the Miraculous Outing: A three-day bacchanalia, celebrating the day k.d. lang came out.

▼ The Ascension: The day Djuna Barnes passed from this world to the great lesbian salon in the sky.

▼ Mother Superior Day: Celebration of dominant women, interdenominational.

## European or Gay?

Observant lesbians who live in places where European tourists visit have discovered a curious and perhaps meaningful phenomenon among the visiting womenfolk: They all look like dykes. Short hair, spectacles, jeans, big black clunky shoes. The more sporting among the American women have devised a game with a dual purpose in mind: to separate the "girls" from the women, and to then meet those who make the cut.

### Rules:

1. Pick out unknown suspect(s). Observe.

2. Ask her/them the time. You'll probably have your answer right there. (If they have an accent . . . )

2a. If European, engage them in a conversation about their trip. If any of the sisterly landmarks crop up, you may have some European lesbians on your hands.[1]

3. If their accents don't take you back to the Old Country, chat them up. Use caution however, as they may merely be straight women from Cleveland, who look just like Midwestern lesbians. Go figure.

4. Make dates. Exchange addresses. Go to Paris tomorrow.

Bets can be taken to liven this up—loser has to buy gifts for the winner. As of this writing, there is no "strip" version of this game.

---

[1] Or you may have some very confused Europeans. If you're wondering what European lesbians look like, they are akin to American supermodels. (Really. No kidding. We've seen them.)

# Ex-Girlfriend Olympics

**Rules:**

1. Go to a party where at least one ex-girlfriend is present; ideally two. Bonus points are awarded if:
   you bring your current girlfriend +10
   ex-girlfriends know each other +20
   ex-girlfriends were dating each other when you met them, and on their break up, you dated both sequentially +50

2. Become just inebriated enough to loosen your tongue. If in recovery, the stress of being there can be enough.

3. Move between various groups of people, noting with good humor the presence of exes.

4. Talk to exes in chronological order; i.e., most recent last. Pretend that you're perfectly okay with this:
   if they broke up with you +20
   if you broke up with them, but really are okay +10 for guts
   if you feel like you've make a mistake and start groveling −20

5. Maneuver exes to talk to each other. Make sure they know what the deal is. If:
   they go home together, you win
   they have a really big screaming match +20
   a drink is thrown +30
   one runs out +40
   fists fly +50 for conflict, but −50 for being an instigator, so 0

6. If they get along, and start talking in loud voices about how you were sloppy, crazy, or bad in bed, they get 1000 points each, and you get what you deserve.

# Name That Vegetarian Meat Substitute!

**Rules:**

1. Create a dish made with one of the various non-meat products available. You should do your best to disguise it by using spices, sauces, and many vegetables.

2. Call friends over for an impromptu dinner party.

3. Feed them.

4. Make them guess what they've just eaten.

5. Whoever guesses first gets the leftovers.

# Spin the Bottle

This doesn't really need any explanation, does it?

# Seven Minutes in Heaven

Same as the Teenage Heterosexual Version, except that after their seven minutes, each participant has to have a crisis about what it meant, e.g., "Do I have to tell my therapist?" "Do we have to date now?"

## Not-a-Lesbian:

This young man is exactly what it says: not a lesbian. The frequent confusion by the uneducated and the unobservant often leads to a completely sullen demeanor. His identity has been subsumed by "lesbian chic," and he has become silenced by the wave of dyke awareness around—making it difficult to live his life, much less actually get a date. Help him, and others like him—think before you speak (helpful hint—check for an Adam's apple or razor stubble before asking for a date).

# LESBIAN STUDIES

OR

CRIB SHEETS FOR A LIFE-STYLE

Lesbian studies, what a concept! When is a dildo not a dildo? When Judith Butler, the high diva of gender theory calls it the "lesbian phallus" and writes a thirty-plus page homage to it, without ever once telling her readers what exactly it is she wants to "possess." Just sit down and try to describe the concept of fluid identities to someone and you'll see there are definite problems. Here is a list of texts that can start you on the path to dyke scholarship.

## What Is a Lesbian?

*Compulsory Heterosexuality and Lesbian Existence*, Adrienne Rich
"Lesbianism: An Act of Resistance," Cheryl Clarke in *This Bridge Called My Back: Writing by Radical Women of Color*—edited by Cherríe Moraga and Gloria Anzaldúa
*Girlfriend Number One: Lesbian Life in the 90s*, edited by Robin Stevens
*Sisters, Sexperts, Queers: Beyond the Lesbian Nation*, edited by Arlene Stein

## History

*Cherry Grove, Fire Island: Sixty Years in America's First Gay and Lesbian Town*, Esther Newton
*Odd Girls and Twilight Lovers* and *Surpassing the Love of Men,* Lillian Faderman
*Boots of Leather, Slippers of Gold: The History of a Lesbian Community*, Elizabeth Lapovsky Kennedy and Madeline D. Davis

## Pornography/Sexuality

*Pleasure and Danger, Exploring Female Sexuality*, edited by Carole S. Vance

*Powers of Desire, The Politics of Sexuality*, edited by Ann Snitow, Christine Stansell, and Sharon Thompson

*Caught Looking*, edited by the Caught Looking Collective

*How Do I Look? Queer Film & Video*, the Bad Object-Choices Collective

*Skin: Talking About Sex, Class and Literature*, Dorothy Allison

*Public Sex: The Culture of Radical Sex*, Pat Califia

Any Book by Susie Bright

*Coming to Power*, the SAMOIS Collective

*Against Sadomasochism: A Radical Feminist Analysis*, edited by Vanya Burstyn and Robin Ruth Linden

## Butch/Femme

*Gender Trouble* and *Bodies That Matter: On the Discursive Limits of Sex*, Judith Butler

*Towards a Butch/Femme Aesthetic*, Sue-Ellen Case

*Vested Interests: Cross-Dressing and Cultural Anxiety*, Marjorie Garber

*The Persistent Desire: A Femme-Butch Reader*, edited by Joan Nestle

*Dagger: On Butch Women*, edited by Lily Burana, Roxxie, and Linnea Due

## FIVE LESBIAN CHILDHOOD HEROES FROM CHILDREN'S BOOKS:

1. Harriet the Spy
2. Ramona the Pest
3. The Pokey Little Puppy
4. Frances the Badger
5. Nancy Drew (duh!)

# Gender Theory

*Gender Trouble* and *Bodies That Matter,* Judith Butler
*Technologies of Gender* and *The Practice of Love,* Teresa De Lauretis
*A Cyborg Manifesto,* Donna Haraway
*A World of Difference,* Barbara Johnson
*In Other Words,* Gayatri Chakoravorty Spivak
*Inside/Out: Lesbian Theories, Gay Theories,* edited by Diana Fuss
The "Queer Theory: Lesbian and Gay Sexualities" issue of *differences*
The "Essays in Lesbian and Gay Studies" issue of *Discourses*
*The Lesbian Postmodern,* edited by Laura Doane
*The Apparitional Lesbian: Female Homosexuality and Modern Culture,*
  Terry Castle
*Lesbian Utopics,* Annemarie Jagose
*Gender Outlaw: On Men, Women, and the Rest of Us,* Kate Bornstein


# Madonna (Cultural) Studies

*The Madonna Connection: Representational Politics, Subcultural Identi-
  ties and Cultural Theory,* edited by Cathy Schwictenberg
*Madonnarama: Essays on Sex and Popular Culture,* edited by Lisa Frank
  and Paul Smith
*Desperately Seeking Madonna,* edited by Adam Sexton
*I Dream of Madonna: Women's Dreams of the Goddess of Pop,* edited
  by Kay Turner


# Separatism

*Lesbian Ethics,* Sarah Lucia Hoagland
*The Lesbian Body, The Straight Mind,* and *The Mark of Gender,* Monique
  Wittig
*Amazon Odyssey,* Ti-Grace Atkinson
*The Dialectic of Sex: The Case for Feminist Revolution,* Shulamith Fire-
  stone
*Lesbian Nation: The Feminist Solution,* Jill Johnston
*Sappho was a Right-On Woman,* edited by Sidney Abbott and Barbara
  Love

# Lit Crit

*Anything,* Catharine Stimpson
*Crack Wars: Literature Addiction Mania,* Avital Ronell
*New French Feminisms,* edited by Isabelle de Courtivin and Elaine
 Marks
*Newly Born Women,* Helene Cixous and Catherine Clement
*The Poetics of Gender,* edited by Nancy K. Miller
*New Lesbian Criticism: Literary and Cultural Readings,* edited by Sally
 Munt

# Lesbians of Color/Ethnicity

*Ain't I a Woman: Black Women and Feminism,* bell hooks
*This Bridge Called My Back: Writing by Radical Women of Color,* edited
 by Cherríe Moraga and Gloria Anzaldúa
*Sister Outsider,* Audre Lorde
*Yours in Struggle,* Barbara Smith, Elly Bulkin, and Minnie Bruce Pratt
*Nice Jewish Girls,* edited by Evelyn Torton Beck
*Borderland/La Frontera: The New Mestiza,* Gloria Anzaldúa (and her
 other works)

# FINAL EXAM

## I. Multiple Choice Questions (35% of total score)

**1. If all the closeted models in America were kidnapped . . .**

    A.  America would be a better place.
    B.  The price of clothing would drop dramatically.
    C.  Calvin Klein would be out of business.
    D.  All of the above.

**2. An essential part of any lesbian wardrobe is:**

    A.  A pair of worn 501s
    B.  A bitchin' coif
    C.  A cute girlfriend
    D.  A big stick

**3. The seminal lesbian novel of the 20th century is:**

    A.  *Nightwood* by Djuna Barnes
    B.  *Rubyfruit Jungle* by Rita Mae Brown
    C.  *Once Is Not Enough,* by Jacqueline Susann
    D.  All of the above

**4. Which answer best completes the phrase: "Ex-girlfriends should . . ."**

    A.  Be sent to a desert island upon breakup, where they will be forced to live out their lives among people as vain and selfish as themselves.
    B.  Never be counted out on a cold lonely night.
    C.  Disappear.
    D.  Be forced to wear a big scarlet letter denoting their crime, to warn other lesbians.

### 5. Complete this sentence: "I love . . ."

A. Martina.
B. My universal sisters, both animal and human.
C. Pussy.
D. A girl in uniform.

## II. Analogies (35% of total score)

### 1. Lea DeLaria::Ellen DeGeneres as Lynn Breedlove::

A. Whitney Houston
B. Alanis Morissette
C. Madonna
D. Dionne Warwick

### 2. Janet Reno::Hillary Rodham Clinton as Gertrude Stein::

A. Alice B. Toklas
B. Elizabeth Bishop
C. Djuna Barnes
D. Your Mother

### 3. Urvashi Vaid::Andrew Sullivan as Candace Gingrich::

A. Bruce Bawer
B. Larry Kramer
C. Gertrude Himmelfrab
D. Your girlfriend

### 4. Hot Sex::True Love as Money::

A. Trouble
B. Pre-domestic partnership agreement
C. Power
D. Looks

**5. Monogamy::Relationship as Beauty::**

    A. Truth
    B. Pain
    C. Art
    D. Beast

## III. Essay Questions (30% of total score)

1. Explain the rise and fall of Ingrid Casares, girl toy to the stars (e.g., k.d. lang, Madonna).
2. Compare and contrast Amy Carter and Chelsea Clinton as both American symbols and feminist icons.
3. Explain and reflect on the phenomena of "dyke tykes" (straight men who pal around with lesbians), "straight queers" (heterosexuals who identify as queer, without the benefit of sleeping with members of the same sex), and "lesbians who sleep with men" (self-explanatory).

## Extra Credit (20 points)

Discuss the symbolism of any three of the following icons, examining their meaning in lesbian culture and their subversive qualities vis a vis heterosexual society:

▼ The Latina Marine, Vasquez, from *Aliens*

▼ Tina Landis, Janet Jackson's choreographer and backup dancer

▼ Olivia Newton-John as she appeared in the movie version of *Grease*

▼ Dee from "What's Happening!"

▼ Nellie Olsen from "Little House on the Prairie"

## Scoring

In the tradition of alternative higher education institutions, this test is not graded. (Hah, fooled you.) The experience of taking this test is an education in itself. Be assured that if you've make it this far, you're going to do just fine.

The future of our people is filled with both great promise and ominous threats. By the time this is published, Americans will be deep in the throes of what promises to be a heated national election. As much fun as it is to be "on the team," there are responsibilities that come with the territory. It's important for you to do your part to help make your city, town, or trailer park safe for your sisters and brothers.

In the name of all that is good and woman-centered, we wish you well on your journey through this world, and simply say: "Vaya con Gaia."

# Resource Guide

## National Lesbian, Gay, and Bisexual Groups (Including National Hotlines, Switchboards, etc.)

American Indian Gays and
Lesbians
P.O. Box 10229
Minneapolis, MN 55458–3229

Asian/Pacific Lesbian and Gays,
Inc.
Box 433 Suite 109
7985 Santa Monica Blvd.
West Hollywood, CA
90046–5111

Gay and Lesbian Arabic Society
Box 4971
Washington, DC 20008

Gay, Lesbian and Bisexual Youth
Hotline
(800) 347-TEEN
Hours: Thurs–Sun 8–12:45
(Eastern)

Hetrick-Martin Institute
2 Astor Place
NY, NY 10003
(212) 674-2400,
TTY (212) 674-8895
Social service agency for gay,
lesbian, and bisexual youth.

National Coalition for Black
Gays and Lesbians
P.O. Box 19248
Washington, DC 20036

National Gay and Lesbian Task
Force
1734 14th St., NW
Washington, DC 20009–4309
(202) 332-6438

National Latino/a Lesbian and
Gay Organization
P.O. Box 44483
Washington, DC 20026
(202) 544-0092

National Runaway Switchboard
(800) 621-4000
Hours: 24 hrs, 7 days a week
Not lesbian/gay/bisexual specific but can provide assistance
to homeless youth of all sexual
orientations as well as crisis intervention, suicide counseling,
and referrals.

Parents and Friends of Lesbians
and Gays (PFLAG)
P.O. Box 27605
Washington, DC 20038
(202) 638-4200
Has chapters across the country. Call or write for nearest
group, literature, and referrals.

Planned Parenthood Federation of
America
(800) 230-7526
This number will automatically
switch you to the clinic closest
to your area. Best to call during
regular business hours.

Hotlines or contact numbers for
groups offering assistance to
battered women and rape vic-
tims are often found in the front
pages of your local white or
yellow pages, by calling your
local police department, or directory information operator.

## State-by-State Listing of Local Switchboards and Lesbian/Gay/Bi/Women's Centers

Listed below are contact numbers for at least one group in each of the fifty states that will be able to provide you with more information about what lesbian, bisexual, or women's groups exist in your area. Most switchboards answer calls during limited hours, generally in the early to late evening, therefore, if you do not get an answer, try again at a later time. For the most comprehensive listing of lesbian and bi groups in the U.S. look for the *Gayellow Pages* and *Places of Interest to Women*.

### Alabama

Gay/Lesbian Information Line of
    Lambda Resource Center
(205) 326-8600, TDD avail
Hours: 6–10 P.M. daily
Correspondence: P.O. Box
    55913, Birmingham, AL 35255
Walk in: Lambda Resource
    Center, 205 32nd St., South

Mobile Area Lesbian & Gay
    Assembly
P.O. Box 40326
Mobile, AL 36640–0326
(205) 450-0501

### Alaska

Gay/Lesbian Helpline of Identity
    Inc.
(907) 258–4777

Alaska Women's Resource Center
111 W Ninth Ave
Anchorage, AK 99501
(907) 276-0528

### Arizona

Lesbian Resource Project of the
    Tempe Women's Center
P.O. Box 26031
Tempe, AZ 85285–6031
(602) 966-6152 (v/TDD)

Lesbian/Gay Community
    Switchboard
(602) 234-2752
(602) 234-0873 (TDD)
P.O. Box 16423
Phoenix, AZ 85011

Wingspan: Tucson's Lesbian, Gay
    and Bisexual Community
    Center
422 N 4th Ave.
Tucson, AZ 85705
(602) 624-1779

### Arkansas

Arkansas Gay and Lesbian Task
    Force Switchboard
(501) 666-3340 in Little Rock
(800) 448-8305 Statewide
Hours: 6:30–10:30 P.M. daily

Women's Project
2224 Main St.
Little Rock, AK 72206
(501) 372-5113

### California

*Berkeley*

Pacific Center for Human Growth
Switchboard: (510) 841-6224
Hours: 10 A.M.–10 P.M. daily
Walk in: 2712 Telegraph Ave.
Berkeley, CA 94705
Phone: (510) 548-8283

**Gay United Services, Inc.**
Switchboard: (204) 268-3541
Correspondence: Box 4640,
Fresno, CA 93744
Walk in: Community Center, 625
N Palm

*Long Beach*

One in Long Beach
Switchboard: (310) 434-4455
Walk in: The Center 2017 E
   Fourth St.
Long Beach, CA 90814

*Los Angeles Area*

Gay and Lesbian Community
   Services Center
1213 N Highland Ave
Los Angeles, CA 90038
(213) 464-7400
(213) 464-0029 (TDD)

South Bay Lesbian and Gay
   Community Center
20009 Artesia Blvd., Suite A
Redondo Beach, CA 90278
(310) 379-2850

*Orange County*

Gay and Lesbian Community
   Services Center of Orange
   County
Hotline: (714) 534-3261,
TDD 534-3441
12832 Garden Grove Blvd., #A
Garden Grove, CA 92643
phone: (714) 534-0862

*Pasadena*

Aloft (Women's Center)
2047 Huntington Drive, #C
South Pasadena, CA
91030–4950
(818) 441-1789

*Sacramento*

Lambda Community Center
Walk in: 1931 L St
(916) 442-0185, 447-5755

El Dorado Women's Center
3133 Gilmore St.
Placerville, CA 95667
(916) 626-1450, 626-1131

Sacramento Women's Center
1924 T St.
Sacramento, CA 95814–6822
(916) 736-6942

*San Bernardino*

Gay & Lesbian Center, Inland
   Empire
(909) 884-5447 6:30–10 P.M.
Correspondence: P.O. Box 6333,
San Bernardino, CA 92412

*San Diego*

Lesbian & Gay Men's Community
   Center
Info line: (619) 692-GAYS
Walk in: 3916 Normal St.
Phone: 692-2077

Center for Women's Studies and
   Services
2467E St.
San Diego, CA 92102
phone: (619) 223-8984
Crisis Hotline: (619) 233-3088

*San Francisco*

Bay Area Youth Switchboard
(415) 386-GAYS

San Francisco Sex Information
(415) 621-7300 Mon–Fri
3–9 P.M.

Women's Building
3543 Eighteenth St.
San Francisco, CA 94110
(415) 431-1180

### San José

Gay & Lesbian Switchboard
(408) 293-4525

Billy De Frank Lesbian and Gay
   Community Center
175 Stockton Ave.
San José, CA 95126-2760
(408) 293-4525

### San Luis Obispo

Women's Resource Center
1009 Morro St. #201
San Luis Obispo, CA
93401–3227
(805) 544-9313

### Santa Barbara Area

Gay & Lesbian Resource Center
126 E Haley #A-17
Santa Barbara, CA 93101
(805) 963-3636

## Colorado

### Colorado Springs

Pikes Peak Gay and Lesbian
   Community Center
Helpline: (719) 471-4429

### Denver

Gay & Lesbian Community Center
   of Colorado
1245 E. Colfax #125
Denver, CO 80218
(303) 831-6268
Switchboard: (303) 831-1598

### Fort Collins

Lambda Community Center
155 N. College Ave #219
Fort Collins, CO 80524
(303) 221-3247

## Connecticut

### Danbury

Women's Center of Greater
Danbury
2 West St.
Danbury, CT 06810
(203) 731-5200

### Hartford

Gay, Lesbian and Bisexual
   Community Center
1841 Broad St.
Hartford, CT 06114
(203) 724-5542

### New Haven

New Haven Women's Liberation
   Center
614 Orange St.
New Haven, CT 06511
(203) 776-2658

### Norwich

Infoline of Eastern Connecticut
(203) 886-0516, 388-9941,
456-8886, 774-7527, 928-6577
Hours: 8–9 P.M., M–F
74 W Main St.
Norwich, CT 06360

### Stamford

Gay and Lesbian Guideline
P.O. Box 8185
Stamford, CT 06905
(203) 327-0767

## Delaware

Gay and Lesbian Alliance of
  Delaware
800 West St.
Wilmington, DE 19801
(302) 655-5280
Hotline: (800) 292-0492

## District of Columbia

Washington Area Gay & Lesbian
  Hotline of the Whitman-Walker
  Clinic
(202) 833-3234
Spanish: 332-2192 (Thu only)

Sexual Minority Youth Assistance
  League (SMYAL)
333 1/2 Pennsylvania Ave. SE
3rd Fl.
Washington, DC 20003
(202) 546-5940
Helpline: (202) 546-5911

## Florida

### Fort Lauderdale

Gay/Lesbian Community Center
P.O. Box 4567
Fort Lauderdale, FL 33338
(305) 763-1530

### Fort Myers

SW Florida Support
(813) 332-2272

### Gainesville

Gay Switchboard
(904) 332-0700

### Miami

Gay, Lesbian and Bisexual
  Community Hotline of
  Greater Miami
(305) 759-3661
24 hrs, but requires a touch tone
phone

Switchboard of Miami
(305) 358-HELP

The Lesbian, Gay and Bisexual
  Community Center
1335 Alton Rd.
(305) 531-3666

### Orlando

Gay/Lesbian Community Services
  of Central Florida
714 E. Colonial Dr.
Office: (407) 425-4527
Hotline: (407) 843-4297 (24 hrs)

### Saint Petersburg

The Line
(813) 586-4297

### Tallahassee

Women's Info Line
(904) 656-7884

### Tampa

Gay Hotline
(813) 229-8839

### West Palm Beach

Compass, Inc.
2677 Forest Hill Blvd.
#106
West Palm Beach, FL 33405
Office: (407) 966-3050
Hotline: (407) 966-3777 (24 hrs)

### Georgia

Atlanta Gay Center
63 12th St.
Atlanta, GA 30309
Office: (404) 876-5372
Helpline: (404) 892-9661,
TDD avail.

### Hawaii

Gay Community Directory
(808) 521-6000

#### Honolulu

Gay & Lesbian Community Center
1820 University Ave.
2nd fl.
Honolulu, HI 96801
(808) 951-7000

### Idaho

The Community Center (TCC)
P.O. Box 323
Boise, ID 83701
(208) 336-3870

### Illinois

#### Champaign/Urbana

Lesbian, Gay, Bisexual
Switchboard
(217) 384-8040

#### Chicago

In Touch Hotline
(312) 996-5535

Horizons Community Services
961 W. Montana
Chicago, IL 60614
Office: (312) 472-6469

Lesbian/Gay Helpline:
(312) 929-HELP, TDD 327-HELP

Lesbian and Gay Community
Center of Chicago
2863 N. Clark St.
Chicago, IL 60657
(312) 666-5300

Chicago Runaway Switchboard
3080 N. Lincoln
Chicago, IL 60657
(800) 621-3230

#### Evanston

Kinheart Women's Center
2214 Ridge Ave.
Evanston, IL 60201
(708) 491-1103

### Indiana

#### Bloomington

Gay and Lesbian Switchboard
(812) 855-5OUT

#### Fort Wayne

Gay/Lesbian Helpline
(219) 744-1199

Gay/Lesbian Resource Center
and Archives at the Up the
Stairs Community Center
3426 Broadway
Fort Wayne, IN 46807
(219) 744-1199

#### Indianapolis

Gay/Lesbian Switchboard/
Community Referral Service
(317) 639-5937

Indianapolis Youth Group Teen
Hotline
(800) 347-TEEN

## Iowa

### Ames

Gay & Lesbian Infoline
(515) 294-2104

American Red Cross Open Line
(515) 233-5000

### Des Moines

Gay & Lesbian Resource Center
4211 Grand Ave.
Des Moines, IA 50312
Infoline: (515) 277-1454
Office: (515) 279-2110

Young Women's Resource Center
554 Twenty-Eighth St.
(515) 224-4901

### Iowa City

Lesbian, Bi, Gay Line
(319) 335-3251

Women's Resource and Action
Center
130 N. Madison
Iowa City, IA 52245
(319) 335-1486

## Kansas

Flint Hills Alliance: Gay, Lesbian,
Bisexual Info Line
P.O. Box 2018
Manhattan, KS 66502
(913) 587-0016

Gay Rap Telephone Line of
Topeka
P.O. Box 223
Topeka, KS 66601
(913) 233-6558
Hours: daily, 9 P.M.–midnight

Wichita Gay Info
(316) 269-0913

## Kentucky

Lexington Gay/Lesbian Services
Organization
(606) 231-0335

## Louisiana

Lesbian & Gay Community Center
of New Orleans
816 N. Rampart St.
New Orleans, LA 70172
(504) 522-1103

## Maine

Gay/Lesbian Phoneline
c/o Box 990
Caribou, ME 04736
(207) 498-2088

## Maryland

Gay and Lesbian Community
Center
241 W. Chase St.
Baltimore, MD 21201
G&L Switchboard:
(410) 837-8888, TDD 837-8525
Office: (410) 837-5445

## Massachusetts

### Amherst area

Gay & Lesbian Info Services
(413) 731-5403

Women's Services Center
146 First St.
Pittsfield, MA 01201
Office: (413) 449-2425
Hotline: (413) 443-0089 (24 hrs)

Boston Gay & Lesbian Helpline
(617) 267-9001 (voice and TTY)

Bisexual Community Resource
Center
P.O. Box 609
Cambridge, MA 02140
(617) 338-9585

Lesbian and Gay Community
Center
P.O. Box 69
West Medford, MA 02156
(617) 247-2927

Women's Center
46 Pleasant St.
Cambridge, MA 02139
(617) 354-8807 (voice and TTY)

## Michigan

*Detroit*

Affirmations
195 W Nine Mile Road,
Suite 110
Ferndale, MI 48220
Office: (313) 398-7105
Switchboard: (313) 398-4297

*Grand Rapids*

Lesbian and Gay Community
Network of Western Michigan
909 Cherry St SE
Grand Rapids, MI 49506
(616) 458-3511

## Minnesota

*Duluth*

Aurora: A Northland Lesbian
Center
8 N Second Ave. E #210
Duluth, MN 55802
(218) 722-4903

*Minneapolis area*

Gay and Lesbian-Hotline
(612) 822-8661; in the upper
midwest (800) 800-0907

Brian Coyle Community Center
420 15th Ave S
Minneapolis, MN 55454
(612) 338-5283

Chrysalis: A Center for Women
2650 Nicollet Ave
Minneapolis, MN 55408
(612) 871-0118 and 871-2603

## Mississippi

Community Services Network
P.O. Box 7737
Jackson, MS 39284
Action Line: (601) 373-8610

*Biloxi*

GL Friendly
308 Caivllavet St.
Biloxi, MS 39530
(601) 435-2398

## Missouri

*Columbia*

Lesbian and Gay Helpline
(314) 449-4477

### Kansas City

Kansas City Gay Talk
P.O. Box 32592
Kansas City, MO 64111
(816) 931-4470

### Saint Charles

The Women's Center
P.O. Box 51
Saint Charles, MO 63302
(314) 946-6854

### Saint Louis

Gay and Lesbian Hotline
(314) 367-0084

The Center
Box 4589
Saint Louis, MO 63108
(314) 997-9897

Women's Self Help Center
2838 Olive St.
Saint Louis, MO 63103
(314) 531-9100 and 531-2003

## Montana

### Bozeman

Lambda Alliance of Gay Men &
   Lesbians
c/o Women's Center
Hamilton Hall #15
Bozeman, MT 59717
(406) 994-3836

### Missoula

Lambda Alliance
(406) 523-5567

## Nebraska

### Lincoln

Gay and Lesbian Youth Talkline
P.O. Box 94882
Lincoln, NE 68502
(402) 479-7932

Lesbian Discussion Group
Women's Center
340 Nebraska Union
Lincoln, NE 68588
(402) 472-2597

### Omaha

Queer Nation
P.O. Box 34463
Omaha, NE 68134
(402) 451-7987

## Nevada

Gay Switchboard
(702) 733-9990

The Center
P.O. Box 60301
(702) 733-9800

## New Hampshire

Gay Info Line of New Hampshire
26 S Main St.
Box 181
Concord, NH 03361
(603) 224-1686

## New Jersey

Gay Helpline of NJ
(201) 692-1794

Morris County Gay Activists
   Alliance Gay Helpline
(201) 285-1595

Jersey Shore Gay and Lesbian
Community Center
529 Bangs Ave. #7
Asbury Park, NJ 07712
(908) 493-0730

*New Brunswick*

Women's Support and Survival
56 College Ave.
New Brunswick, NJ 08903
(908) 828-7273

**New Mexico**

*Albuquerque*

Common Bond
4013 Silver Rd. SE
Gay and Lesbian Info Line:
(505) 266-8041

**New York**

*Albany area*

Capital District Lesbian & Gay
Community Center
332 Hudson Ave
Albany, NY 12201
(518) 462-6138

Women's Building
79 Central Ave
Albany, NY 12206
(518) 465-1597

*Binghamton*

The S.P.A.C.E
213 State St.
Binghamton, NY 13901
(607) 724-2582
Event line: (607) 724-3462

*Buffalo*

Gay and Lesbian Youth Services
190 Franklin St.
Buffalo, NY 14202
Hotline: (716) 855-0221

*New York City area*

Gay and Lesbian Switchboard of
Long Island
(516) 737-1615

Westchester Gay and Lesbian
Help-Line
(914) 948-4922

Lesbian Switchboard
(212) 741-2610

New York City Gay/Lesbian
Anti-Violence Project
(212) 807-0197, (24 hrs)

Lesbian and Gay Community
Services Center
208 W 13th St.
NY, NY 10011
(212) 620-7310

Shades of Lavender
295 9th St.
Brooklyn, NY 11215
(718) 499-0352

The Loft: Lesbian and Gay
Community Services Center
255 Grove St.
White Plains, NY 10601
(914) 984-4922

Women's Alternatives Community
Center
669 Woodfield Rd.
West Hempstead, NY 11552
(516) 483-2050

Reachout of St. Lawrence County
P.O. Box 5051
Potsdam, NY 13676
Hotline: (315) 265-2422

*Rochester*

Gay Alliance of Genessee Valley
179 Atlantic Ave
Rochester, NY 14607
(716) 244-8640

*Syracuse*

Gayline
P.O. Box 738
Syracuse, NY 13201
(315) 422-5732

Gayphone
c/o Gay, Lesbian, Bisexual
Student Assoc.
750 Ostrom Ave
Syracuse, NY 13244
(315) 443-3599

Women's Information Center
601 Allen St.
Syracuse, NY 13210
(315) 478-4636


**North Carolina**

*Asheville*

Asheville Gay & Lesbian Info Line
c/o SALGA
P.O. Box 197
Asheville, NC 28802
(704) 253-2971

Gay & Lesbian Helpline of Wake
County
(919) 821-0055

Our Own Place (lesbian center,
but all women welcome)
P.O. Box 11732
Durham, NC 27703
(919) 688-0233

The Women's Center
210 Henderson St.
Chapel Hill, NC 27514
(919) 968-4610

*Charlotte*

Gay/Lesbian Switchboard of
Charlotte
P.O. Box 11144
Charlotte, NC 28220
(704) 535-6277 (TDD avail.)

Women's Center
P.O. Box 8058
Charlotte, NC 28203
(704) 334-9655

*Greensboro*

Alternative Resources of the Triad
P.O. Box 4442
Greensboro, NC 27404
Office: (910) 275-1834
Gay and Lesbian Hotline:
(910) 274-2100

*Wilmington*

Gay & Lesbian Switchboard
c/o GROW
341–11 S. College Rd. #182
Wilmington, NC 28403
(910) 675-9222

### North Dakota

FMGA
(701) 232-6032
weekly gay dances

### Ohio

*Cincinnati*

Gay and Lesbian Community
  Switchboard
P.O. Box 141061
Cincinnati, OH 45250
(513) 651-0070

Greater Cincinnati Gay/Lesbian
  Center
P.O. Box 141061
Cincinnati, OH 45250
(513) 651-0040

*Cleveland*

Lesbian and Gay Community
  Center of Greater Cleveland
1418 W. Twenty-Ninth
Cleveland, OH 44113
Office: (513) 522-1999
Lesbian/Gay Hotline:
(513) 781-6736

Women's Building Project
3130 Mayfield Rd.
Cleveland, OH 44118
(513) 321-3054

Womenspace
1101 Euclid Ave.
Cleveland, OH 44115
Helpline: (513) 696-3100

*Columbus*

Stonewall Community Center
47 W. Fifth Ave.
Columbus, OH 43201
(614) 299-7764, 299-4408
(Fax and TTY)

*Lorain*

Lorain Lesbian/Gay Center
P.O. Box 167
Lorain, OH 44052
(216) 960-2050

*Mentor*

Mentor Center (HUGS East)
P.O. Box 253
Mentor, OH 44061
(216) 974-8909

### Oklahoma

*Oklahoma City*

Oasis Resource Center
2135 NW 39th St.
Oklahoma City, OK 73112
(405) 525-2437

Herland Sister Resources
2132 NW 39th St.
Oklahoma City, OK 73112
(405) 521-9696

Women's Resource Center
226 E. Gray
Norman, OK 73070
(405) 364-9424, 360-0590

*Tulsa*

TOHR Gay/Lesbian Helpline
P.O. Box 52729
Tulsa, OK 74152
(918) 743-GAYS

## Oregon

### Bend

The GALON (Gay and Lesbian
   Outreach Network)
P.O. Box 5672
Bend, OR 97708
(503) 388-2395 (24 hrs)

### Portland

Phoenix Rising
620 SW 5th Ave #710
Portland, OR 97204
(513) 223-8299

### Roseburg

Gay & Lesbian Switchboard
(513) 672-4126

## Pennsylvania

### Altoona

Gay, Lesbian & Bisexual Helpline
c/o Family & Children's Service
2022 Broad Ave.
Altoona, PA 16601
(814) 942-8101

### Harrisburg

Gay & Lesbian Switchboard of
   Harrisburg
P.O. Box 872
Harrisburg, PA 17108
(717) 234-0328

### Philadelphia

Philadelphia Gay Switchboard
P.O. Box 2091
Philadelphia, PA 19103
(215) 546-7100

Tell-A-Woman
1530 Locust St.
Box 322
Philadelphia, PA 19102
(215) 564-5810

Penguin Place: Gay/Lesbian
   Community Center of
   Philadelphia
210 S. Camac St.
Philadelphia, PA 19107
(215) 732-2220

### Pittsburgh

Gay & Lesbian Community Center
   of Pittsburgh
2214 E. Carson St.
(412) 422-0114

### State College

Gay & Lesbian Switchboard
P.O. Box 805
State College, PA 16804
(814) 237-1950

Women's Resource Center
140 W. Nittany Ave
State College, PA 16801
Office: (814) 234-5222
Hotline: (814) 234-5050 (24 hrs)

### Williamsport

Gay & Lesbian Switchboard of
   North Central Pennsylvania
P.O. Box 2510
Williamsport, PA 17703
(717) 327-1141

## Rhode Island

Gay/Lesbian Helpline of Rhode
   Island
P.O. Box 5671
Providence, RI 02903
(401) 751-3322

## South Carolina

The Center
P.O. Box 12648
Columbia, SC 29211
(803) 325-GAYS

## South Dakota

The Coalition
P.O. Box 89803
Sioux Falls, SD 57105
(605) 333-0603

## Tennessee

### Knoxville

Gay & Lesbian Hotline
P.O. Box 2343
Knoxville, TN 37901
(615) 521-6546

### Memphis

Gay & Lesbian Switchboard
P.O. Box 41074
Memphis, TN 38174
(901) 728-GAYS

Memphis Gay & Lesbian
  Community Center
1665 Madison Ave.
Memphis, TN 38174
(901) 276-4651

### Nashville

The Center for Lesbian & Gay
  Community Services
703 Berry Rd.
Nashville, TN 37204
(615) 297-0008 (24 hrs)

## Texas

### Dallas/Fort Worth

Gayline
P.O. Box 190835
Dallas, TX 75219
(214) 368-6283

Lesbian Info Line
P.O. Box 191433
Dallas, TX 75219
(214) 528-2426

Gay/Lesbian Community Center
2701 Reagen
Dallas, TX 75219
(215) 528-4233

Lesbian Resource Center
1315 Skiles St.
Dallas, TX 75204
(215) 821-3999

### El Paso

LAMBDA Services
P.O. Box 31321
El Paso, TX 79931
(915) 562-4297

### Houston

Gay & Lesbian Switchboard of
  Houston
P.O. Box 66469
Houston, TX 77266
(713) 529-3211

Crisis Hotline
P.O. Box 130866
Houston, TX 77219
(713) 228-1505

Houston Institute for the Protection
  of Youth
811 Westheimer #210
Houston, TX 77006
(713) 942-YUTH

Houston Area Women's Center
3101 Richmond #150
Houston, TX 77098
(713) 528-2121

*Lubbock*

Community Outreach Center
102 Avenue S
Lubbock, TX 79464
(806) 762-1019

*San Antonio*

LISA (Lesbian Info San Antonio)
P.O. Box 12327
San Antonia, TX 78212
(210) 828-LISA

San Antonio Gay & Lesbian
    Switchboard
Box 120402
San Antonio, TX 78212
(210) 733-7300

The Resource Center
121 W. Woodlawn
San Antonio, TX 78212
(210) 732-0751

**Utah**

Utah Stonewall Center
770 South 300 West
Salt Lake City, UT 84101
(801) 539-8800

Aardvaark Helpline
(801) 533-0927

**Vermont**

Outright Vermont (gay, lesbian
    and bi youth organization)
P.O. Box 5235
Burlington, VT 05402
(802) 865-9677 or
(800) GLB-CHAT

Burlington Women's Council
Room 14 City Hall
Burlington, VT 05401
(802) 865-7200 Tu–Thu 9–5

**Virginia**

*Arlington*

Whitman-Walker Clinic of
Northern Virginia
3426 Washington Blvd. Suite 102
Arlington, VA
Info and hotline: (703) 358-9550

*Charlottesville*

Lesbian & Gay Student Union
    Helpline
(804) 971-4942

*Norfolk*

Gay Information Line
(804) 622-GAYS, 632-BARS

**Washington**

Lesbian Resource Center
1208 E Pine
Seattle, WA 98122
(206) 322-3953 (TTY avail.)

**West Virginia**

Gay & Lesbian Helpline
Morgantown, WV
(304) 292-GAY2

### Wisconsin

*Madison*

The United
14 W. Mifflin St. #103
Madison, WI 53703
Lesbian Line: (608) 255-0743

*Milwaukee*

Gay Info and Services
(414) 444-7331

### Wyoming

United Gays & Lesbians of
   Wyoming
P.O. Box 2037
Laramie, WY 82070
(307) 632-5362

## Zines

There are glossy magazines about
the dyke life that are great, but
there are times when these
lifestyle mags don't even come
close to the boundless joy inspired
by the psychotic excesses of a really rabid rant found in a great
girl zine. The zine scene has really exploded in the last few years
and it is impossible to list all the
zines a girl could read here, so to
find one that will cure what ails
you write to the following distribu-
tors or catalogs:

*Action Girl Newsletter*
c/o Sarah
Box 060456
Staten Island, NY 10304
   Reviews and distributes tons of
   pro-girl zines.

*Factsheet Five*
P.O. Box 170099
San Francisco, CA 94117
   Send $6 for a sample issue.
   The biggest and best known
   listing of the world o' zines.

*Queer Zine Explosion*
c/o Larry-bob
Box 590488
San Francisco, CA 94159–0488
lroberts@bellahs.com
http://www.io.com/~larrybob
   send two stamps for the *Queer
   Zine Explosion*, a catalog of
   queer zines. Also publishes
   *Holy Titclamps*, an excellent
   queer zine.

*Riot Grrrl Press*
1573 N. Milwaukee Ave.
#473
Chicago, IL 60622
   Riot Grrrl Press distributes girl
   zines and info on how to find
   local riot grrrl chapters. Send
   $1 and 2 stamps for a catalog.

## Magazines, Newspapers, Journals

*Aché: A National Journal for Black
Lesbians*
P.O. Box 6071
Albany, CA 94706

*The Advocate*
P.O. Box 4371
Los Angeles, CA 90078–4371

*Bay Windows*
1523 Washington St.
Boston, MA 02118
(617) 266-6670

*B.G. (Black & Gay)*
Box 1511 Cooper Station
NY, NY 10276

BLK
P.O. Box 83912
Los Angeles, CA 90083–0912

*Deneuve: The Lesbian Magazine*
2336 Market St. #15
San Francisco, CA 94114
(415) 863-6538

*Equal Time* Newspaper
310 E 38th St.
#207
Minneapolis, MN 55409
(612) 823-3836

*Girljock*
P.O. Box 882723
San Francisco, CA 94188

*Lesbian Contradiction: A Journal of
Irreverent Feminism*
584 Castro St. #356
San Francisco, CA 94114

*off our backs*
2423 18th St. NW
Washington, DC 20009

*On Our Backs*
526 Castro St.
San Francisco, CA 94114

*Out Magazine*
110 Greene St., #800
New York, NY 10012
(212) 334-9119

*San Francisco Bay Times*
288 7th St.
San Francisco, CA 94103-4004
(415) 626-8121

*San Francisco Sentinel*
285 Shipley
San Francisco, CA 94107
(415) 281-3745

*Southern Voice*
P.O. Box 18215
Atlanta, GA 30316
(404) 876-1819

*The Washington Blade*
1048 U St. NW 2nd Fl
Washington, DC
20009-3916
(202) 797-7000

*Wind City Times*
Sentury Publications
970 W. Montana, #2FL
Chicago, IL 60614
(312) 935-1790

## Books

### Coming Out

Alyson, Sasha, ed. *Young, Gay
and Proud!,* Boston: Alyson 1985.

Holmes, Sarah, ed. *Testimonies: A
Collection of Lesbian Coming Out
Stories,* Boston: Alyson, 1988.

*Bi Any Other Name: Bisexual Peo-
ple Speak Out,* Boston: Alyson,
1991.

### Sexuality

Califia, Pat. *Sapphistry: The Book
of Lesbian Sexuality,* Illustrations by
Tee Corrine, Tallahasse: Naiad
Press, 1980.

Loulan, JoAnn. *Lesbian Sex,* Minneapolis: Spinsters ink, 1984.

Samois Collective. *Coming to
Power: Writings and Graphics on
Lesbian S/M,* Boston: Alyson,
1981.

Sisley, Emily L. and Bertha Harris. *The Joy of Lesbian Sex,* New York: Simon & Schuster, 1977.

## Web Sites for Dykes with Bytes

CyberQueer Lounge
http://sparky.cyberzine.org
   This site features updates on news of interest to queers around the world, and a huge alphabetized list of links to other queer sites and gay and lesbians who are "out" on the web. The bummer is that it contains a warning that is meant to show those under 18 to the door.

Dead Jackie Susann Quarterly
http://www.carroll.com/franny
   Visit the electronic home of our sick and twisted little zine devoted to the patron saint of high camp. Leave us email, tell us how much you hate/love us or just ask who the hell Jacqueline Susann is.

Dyke Action Machine
http://www.echonyc.com/~dam
   A laugh riot from a group of girls always ready for a riot. It's camp, it's fun, I wish I thought of it first! The graphics are bold, beautiful, and well there's nothing not to love about this site.

Factsheet Five Electronic
http://kzsu.stanford.edu/uwi/f5e
   The electronic version of the review to end all reviews of the zine world and beyond.

Holy Titclamps/Queer Zine Explosion
http://www.io.com/~larrybob
   Read Holy Titclamps, or check out the epic list of Queer Zines maintained by Larry-bob, either way, it's a truly awesome site.

Hothead Paisan
http://www.marystreet.com/HH
   She's hot, she's pissed, and she's my dream date! Now Hothead Paisan the Homicidal Lesbian Terrorist is online so I can read an issue or two or just order an issue without leaving the comfort of my cushy abode. It rules . . . go there now, thank me later.

K-Web
http://www.freedom-subdued.org
   K-Web stands for Kinky Women Expanding Boundaries and I quote from the page: "a perverted playground for penisless people and those who love them." Need I say more? I didn't think so.

La Femme
http://www.webcom.com/~femme
   A virtual cafe for lesbians, the site features a cyberbar with home pages for the patrons so that you can pick out the girl of your technodreams to meet and mingle with electronically.

Lesbian Herstory Archives
http://www.intac.com/~kgs/lha
   Get info about the archive, surf a couple links to other dyke centered sites or just view one of the changing online exhibits on lesbian herstory . . . it's a goldmine of info about lesbian lives and loves.

## Lesbian Links

http://www.best.com/~agoodloe

One stop shopping for those of us who are looking for links of interest to girlies who love other girlies. You'll find a list of lesbian focused mailing lists, linked to sites for info about lesbian activism, links to sites about sex and sexuality, links to dyke virtual salons, miscellaneous queer/dyke resource sites and web pages by lesbians. If it's got the word lesbian on it . . . it's in here!

## Muzzy Pages

http://www.jett.com

A site put together by the grrrls who run the queer punk electronic mailing list, this site features info on queer punk bands, the Outpunk page, a link to the Billy De Frank Lesbian and Gay Community Center in San José as well as tons of links to various other punk and activist sites.

## Out Magazine

http://www.out.com

An index of articles that appeared in *Out*, message boards, up-to-second gossip reports, links, and the most popular feature—downloadable pictures of a plethora of boys and girls to get your heart athumping.

## Outproud

http://youth.org/outproud

A really really huge database of gay, lesbian, and bisexual youth groups across the country. Completely anonymous and comprehensive, all you do is enter your zip code and poof! through the magic of technology, seconds later you're provided with a list of contacts in your area.

## Queer Resources Directory

http://www.qrd.org/QRD

With a ton of links and contact numbers, this is another indispensable database of info about queer groups both on and offline.

## Yahoo

http://www.yahoo.com

Yahoo is a monstrously large index to what's what on the web. Go to the society and culture heading then look for the "Gay, Lesbian and Bisexual" subheading and you'll find your way to enough links to exhaust this and your next lifetime.

# ABOUT THE AUTHORS

**Liz Tracey** is the Editor-in-Chief of *LGNY* (Lesbian and Gay New York) and the editor of *A Delicate Fire: Quotations on Lesbian Love* (St. Martin's, 1996.) She was a columnist (with Sydney Pokorny) for *Outweek* magazine, and is a contributor to *Out*. She lives in New York City, where she was born and raised.

**Sydney Pokorny** is a graduate of Vassar College. She currently lives in New York where she is the co-founder and editor of the infrequently published (though still quite alive) zine *Dead Jackie Susann Quarterly*.